The McKinsey *Quarterly*

S0-BFB-937

On the cover

What to do about health care

Why Americans pay more for health care

Diana Farrell, Eric S. Jensen, and Bob Kocher

28

New research from the McKinsey Global Institute and McKinsey's health care practice indicates that health care costs in the United States are $650 billion more than might be expected, given its wealth and the experience of similar countries. Outpatient care—including visits to physicians, same-day hospital treatments, and emergency-room care—is responsible for the largest piece (two-thirds) of the additional spending, followed by drugs and administration and insurance.

It's not clear whether the United States gets $650 billion in extra value. The challenge for reformers is to retain the current system's strengths while addressing its deficiencies and curbing costs.

38
Reader comments on this article from mckinseyquarterly.com

Three imperatives for improving US health care

Paul D. Mango and Vivian E. Riefberg

40

Reforming the US health care system presents daunting challenges. Any reforms must confront its central short-comings: the relentless annual growth in health care costs and the resulting lack of affordable care for much of the population.

To stem these rising costs, the public and private sectors should cooperate to tackle the high incidence of obesity and other chronic behavior-induced diseases, to minimize the economic distortions that impede value-conscious decision making, and to reduce unnecessary administrative complexity.

This article contains two sidebars: "When clinicians lead" and "How health care costs contribute to income disparity in the United States."

Also in this package:

54
Improving Japan's health care system

Nicolaus Henke, Sonosuke Kadonaga, and Ludwig Kanzler

Japan needs the right prescription for providing its citizens with high-quality health care at an affordable price.

Feature articles

High Technology

Marketing

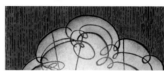

The crisis: Staying ahead of your competitors

**Six ways to make
Web 2.0 work**

Michael Chui, Andy Miller,
and Roger P. Roberts

64

Web 2.0, the latest wave in corporate
technology adoptions, could have
a more far-reaching organizational
impact than technologies adopted
widely in the 1990s, such as enterprise resource planning (ERP),
customer relationship management
(CRM), and supply chain management (SCM). These new tools have a
strong element of bottom-up activity
and demand a mind-set different from
those of earlier IT programs, which
were instituted primarily by edicts from
senior managers. We have identified
six management imperatives to help
companies successfully implement
these technologies.

**Cutting sales costs,
not revenues**

Anupam Agarwal, Eric Harmon,
and Michael Viertler

76

As fear overcomes top management's
natural reluctance to tinker with the
engine that drives revenue, economic
downturns often push companies to
cut their sales force costs.

The outcome, however, can be disas-
trous if companies pay too much
attention to cutting costs quickly and
too little to the consequences of the
measures they adopt.

A sales force can be made better
as well as cheaper—and rapidly, too.
By using the right sales channels
for the right customers, companies
can weather the current storm and
capitalize on opportunities when the
economy rebounds.

Corporate Finance
**Mapping decline and
recovery across sectors**

Bin Jiang, Timothy M. Koller,
and Zane D. Williams

87

Different sectors enter and emerge from
downturns at different times. A look
at past recessions suggests how some
industries may fare.

Operations
**Upgrading R&D in a
downturn**

Christie W. Barrett, Christopher S.
Musso, and Asutosh Padhi

92

Cutting research costs across the board
in a recession isn't smart. Companies
should use R&D as an opportunity to
make themselves more competitive.

High Technology
High tech: Finding opportunity
in the downturn

Andrew Cheung, Eric Kutcher,
and Dilip Wagle

95

In the past, high-tech companies that
made these five kinds of moves
emerged as leaders of the pack when
the economy improved.

Organization

The irrational side of change management

Carolyn Aiken and Scott Keller

100
Thousands of books and articles have been written about change management, and executives increasingly base change programs on sensible principles for influencing attitudes and behavior. Yet, success rates—at around 30 percent—have not improved.

The odds would be much better if change leaders took into account nine counterintuitive insights about how irrational but predictable aspects of human nature sometimes get in the way of successfully applying the building blocks required for behavioral change.

Among the insights: it takes five compelling change "stories"—not one—to motivate employees, and much of the energy that leaders invest in communicating with staff would be better spent listening, not telling.

107
Recommended reading for this article

Financial Services

A Chinese view of governance and the financial crisis: An interview with ICBC's chairman

Dominic Barton, Yi Wang, and Mei Ye

110
Jiang Jianqing, the chairman of the Industrial and Commercial Bank of China (ICBC)—China's largest state-owned lender—argues that efforts to tighten regulation and strengthen governance have helped China's largest lenders minimize their exposure to the global financial crisis. In an interview with McKinsey's Dominic Barton, Yi Wang, and Mei Ye, Jiang notes that the Western governance model isn't the only way of assuring solid financial performance and prudent risk management. Jiang also stresses that the crisis hasn't lessened ICBC's enthusiasm for derivatives and other complex financial products.

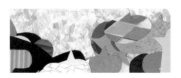

Strategy
Where innovation creates value

Amar Bhidé

119
It doesn't matter where scientific discoveries and breakthrough technologies originate—for national prosperity, the important thing is who commercializes them. The United States is not behind in that race.

Strategy
Market rebels and radical innovation

Hayagreeva Rao

126
Activists play a key role in making or breaking new markets, products, and services. Managers who think like insurgents can shape market acceptance of innovations while stimulating radical change within the organization.

4

Departments

This Quarter

7
A new era for health care

On Our Web Site

8
**Now available on
mckinseyquarterly.com**

Letters to the Editor/
From Our Online
Discussions

10
**Reader responses to
The McKinsey Quarterly,
2009 Number 1**

12
**Reader comments on
our blog post about
the centered-leadership
model**

In Brief
Research and perspectives
on management

14
**Promoting energy
efficiency in
the developing world**

18
Toolbox: Identifying
employee skill gaps

19
The* Quarterly *Surveys

20
***Conversation Starter*:**
Mobilizing boards for change

22
***Speaking of* Strategy:**
An interview
with Alberto Alessi

24
**Management practices
that drive supply chain
success**

Center Stage
A look at current trends and
topics in management

74
**Five trends that will
shape business technology
in 2009**

In Response
Comments from invited experts

134
**Three experts weigh
in on Bill Emmott's article,
"What China can learn
from Japan on cleaning up
the environment"**

Enduring Ideas
Classic McKinsey frameworks
that continue to inform management thinking

140
The business system

This Quarter

A new era for health care

Efforts to reform health care pervade the world's developed economies. Crippling medical-resource constraints express themselves variously as extended wait times, budget overruns, and, in the United States, the rising percentage of the uninsured. As the world enters the third era of modern-health-system management, a combination of technology and unhealthy lifestyles clashes with financial sustainability.

The first era, prompted by the urbanization accompanying the Industrial Revolution in the 18th and 19th centuries, focused on eradicating contagious disease. Great success followed the achievement of proper hygiene (made possible by the development of clean water systems, adequate sewers, and electric motors) and the mass manufacture of vaccines. During the second era, beginning near the turn of the 20th century, stunning technological breakthroughs occurred in areas such as radiology, aseptic surgery, and clinical pathology. These achievements, in turn, led to the institutionalization of medicine in hospitals that eventually required payments from private-sector health insurance and government-sponsored social programs to provide affordable access.

Scientific advances in the practice of medicine over the past century have been nothing short of miraculous, permitting physicians to create and extend life in circumstances that until recently would have been utterly impossible. The pace of scientific change introduces complexity, however, and great variation in the practice of medicine in clinical settings. Meanwhile, the underlying health status of many populations is deteriorating dramatically, largely as a result of changes in lifestyle, behavior, and social norms, as well as the ubiquity of cheap processed foods. The combination of great science and unhealthy lives strains a health system's economic viability. People now live for decades with a variety of expensive-to-treat chronic diseases. For society as a whole, these diseases are neither insurable nor affordable.

So the imperative for this third era of health-system management is behavioral change: healthier lifestyles, to prevent people from making themselves sick, and rigorous practice standards for physicians, transforming their art into a science. Neither governments nor the private sector can achieve these changes independently; public–private partnerships are essential. Governments will play a much more active role as financing agents and as creators of the system's new architecture while the private sector innovates, manages, and executes within it.

These are heady times for leaders of health systems. The challenges and stakes are enormous. We hope that the *Quarterly*'s cover package, focusing on the reform and management of this crucial sector, offers a way forward.

Paul Mango
Director, Pittsburgh office

On Our Web Site

Now available on mckinseyquarterly.com

Join the conversation

These short essays by leading thinkers in their fields, within and outside of McKinsey, are designed to encourage discussion. Read what people are saying, then join the conversation.

Recent conversation starters:

A better way to fix the banks

Here's a plan that could solve the toxic-asset pricing problem voluntarily—without requiring Uncle Sam to nationalize the whole industry—and make (pretty much) everyone a winner.

When job seekers invade Facebook

The increasing popularity of online social networking is changing not only the way people manage their careers but social networking itself.

Join the *McKinsey Quarterly* community on Facebook.

The new normal

The business landscape has changed fundamentally; tomorrow's environment will be different, but no less rich in possibilities for those who are prepared.

Surveys

Measuring marketing:
McKinsey Global Survey Results

Marketing may be hard to measure, but many companies aren't even using the tools available to them. However, some companies with a clearer understanding of their spending are planning to increase it, even in the current economic environment.

Valuing corporate social responsibility: McKinsey Global Survey Results

Environmental, social, and governance programs create shareholder value, most executives believe, but neither CFOs nor professional investors fully include that when evaluating business projects or companies.

Videos and video interactives

Connecting climate change and economic recovery

Economist Nicholas Stern discusses the downturn and its effect on the climate change agenda.

Developing entrepreneurship among the world's poorest

Acumen Fund founder and CEO Jacqueline Novogratz shares stories of social-sector entrepreneurship in an excerpt from her new book, *The Blue Sweater.* A video interview with the author takes you behind the book.

How to fix the innovation gap:
A conversation with Judy Estrin

The author and tech executive says we are living off the fruits of previous research and need to seed new ideas.

Discover What Matters

McKinsey's newest site convenes leading thinkers from around the world, weighing in with scores of essays on topics—from geopolitics to the credit crisis to health care—that will shape our future. We begin with climate change and a discussion among our experts on the merits of a carbon tax versus a cap-and-trade system. Find out what matters, then join the conversation.

whatmatters.mckinseydigital.com

Articles

The CFO's role in navigating the downturn

Companies—and their CFOs—may have to adapt more radically to the downturn than they now expect.

What's different about M&A in this downturn

M&A may be more resilient in this downturn than in previous ones, but it will be a different kind of M&A.

The economic impact of increased US savings

US consumers are spending less and saving more. The economic impact of that combination will depend upon how fast incomes grow.

Opening up to investors

Executives need to embrace transparency if they want to help investors make investment decisions. But what should be disclosed?

Building a flexible supply chain for uncertain times

The "bullwhip effect" means that distortions in data cascade through a company's suppliers. Businesses must remain flexible to protect themselves.

Find us on iTunes

McKinsey Quarterly podcasts, including conversations with authors and readings of articles, are available on iTunes.

listen.to/mckinseyquarterly

Recent podcast:

Hal Varian on how the Web challenges managers

Google's chief economist says executives in wired organizations need a sharper understanding of how technology empowers innovation.

Follow us on Twitter

Receive notifications of new articles by following @McKQuarterly on Twitter.

Put our widget on your page

Our widget allows you to view, read, and share *Quarterly* content on your social network, blog, or personalized page.

Letters to the Editor

Reader responses to *The McKinsey Quarterly*, 2009 Number 1, "The crisis: A new era in management"

Managing regulation in a new era

As concern over global problems mounts, executives and regulators have everything to gain from building relationships based on trust, and developing solutions that benefit a wide range of stakeholders.

You write: "Regulation is about solving problems that society or businesses can't solve alone . . ." But society is not to be opposed to business— the first engulfs the second.

To me, regulation is an act of state institutions (hopefully democratically designated by the citizens) to set rules on dealing with the commons. Regulations don't solve problems; they define a framework and control mechanisms for actions of private and/or public actors. The art of government is to set the right framework so that the well being of the citizens will improve. The art of business is to develop a successful enterprise within this framework.

Of course a collaborative partnership on negotiating and setting regulations is surely better than an arm's length attitude; this is common sense, although some actors show such mistrust for the others that it is not obvious to put it in place.

The current call for more regulation in the financial sector remains vague and has populist tones. Concrete questions are not yet addressed,

explained, and debated: what to regulate, with what aim and how, by whom, and who controls the comptroller? But this is one of many particular issues, and your article does not just deal with regulations, despite its title.

State intervention is different from regulation: in case of crisis, it is done aside of the normal regulatory framework. That is what has now happened in the banking sector and should remain temporary. In a normal case, the political order of a given state and its constitutional frame define what are the areas of direct state intervention (such as defense or schools), those of no state intervention (all the rest, which may include banking or bicycle manufacturing), and what are the grey or mixed zones (for instance, health, farming, or transportation).

Your article deals with political choices and strategies that are of a different kind, not to be confused with regulation or intervention. Wide and profound societal issues such as energy policy, water access, and environmental challenges are at the core of the political debate. They will have a "regulatory" dimension once choices are made. But regulations in these areas are somehow already preempting the choices—influenced by advocate groups of all sorts—including business. This is a kind of collusion between civil servants, business, and NGOs; all insiders and self-designated experts. It is then no surprise that when the public at large is consulted, the outcome may be different than the one expected by the experts. Examples: refusal of the privatization of the electricity business in Switzerland, nonadoption of the Lisbon treaty by the Irish voters, and street demonstrations on GMO in France. Instead of this collusion, a public debate and a direct democracy system like the one of Switzerland are needed; but such a system is perceived as a nemesis by politicians, businesses, and advocacy groups.

Michel de Rougemont
MR-int Enterprise Consulting
Kaiseraugst, Switzerland

Creative destruction and the financial crisis: An interview with Richard Foster

A coauthor of *Creative Destruction* explains how the business world—and the capitalist system—will change in the aftermath of the financial crisis.

I am currently reading Richard Foster's book on innovation and was happy to read his clear and forceful article on the financial crisis and the long view. I am surprised, however, not to see more reference to the need for finding ways of making the financial sector more efficient.

Creative destruction works when it creates more value than it destroys. The financial sector seems to be destroying large amounts of value in a short time—maybe more than it has created—in the financial sector and elsewhere.

As Foster explains, finance does create some value (despite the fact that it does not deal with real assets or bring real satisfaction, as does food, travel, films, and the like). For example, it creates information on real businesses that helps people choose in which companies to invest, and spread their risk.

However, a large part of the financial sector—which is pursuing 15 percent plus return rates, way above the 6 to 7 percent growth of the world economy—is spending huge amounts of resources on a zero-sum game, namely, a rate of return above the 6 to 7 percent real economy growth. It seems a huge waste to spend so much brainpower on a zero-sum game.

Why, if I am right, is this? Is it because the financial sector keeps profits but externalizes losses to the rest of society, thus encouraging inefficient behavior? Is it because it does excessively risky things, like speculating on borrowed money? Or because banks trade on their own account, benefitting from information asymmetries and conflicting interests with their clients?

I would very much like to have Mr. Foster's views on this subject, for I believe finance must be fixed but have seen few good ideas on how to fix the apparent flaws at the root of the present world crisis.

Rui Teixeira Guerra
Darwin Consulting & Finance
Paris, France

Taking improbable events seriously

The author of *The Black Swan* explains why the rarity and unpredictability of certain events does not make them unimportant.

The interview with Mr. Taleb was surely good reading. However, I disagree with the rather blunt dismissal by Mr. Taleb of most of the traditional tools of business and financial management. It appears to me that he ignores the fact that these work quite well most of the time. To me, "black-swan thinking" is to be done in parallel with portfolio and other planning, and needs to be taken seriously.

Mr. Taleb further endorses aggressive risk taking on the positive black swans. Again, I have some reservations, as literally nothing is only good or bad. I am not worried by the financial implications, as Mr. Taleb quite relevantly limits this to those opportunities that "cost you very little." I am, however, worried sick about skewing the attention of management. I have seen too many companies chase multiple "rabbits," in the process ending up empty handed and losing out on the core business and competencies of the company.

This, to me, has the substantial potential of generating a negative black swan out of pursuing the positive ones.

Still, a mind-provoking and truly valuable interview with an authority on thought. Thank you.

Hans Læssøe
Strategic Risk Manager,
LEGO System A/S
Billund, Denmark

(continued on next page)

Strategy in a 'structural break'

During hard times, a structural break in the economy is an opportunity in disguise. To survive—and, eventually, to flourish—companies must learn to exploit it.

"Today, nuclear power, infrastructure repair, and fiber to the home are already on the list of possible stimuli for the economy."

First on my list would be weatherization and insulation for our built environment. It would provide immediate jobs, immediate energy and cost savings, immediate reduction in greenhouse gas pollution, and would reduce the need for new power generation. Then I'd go for industrial and commercial cogeneration, using the new regulatory regime that Thomas Casten of Recycled Energy Development has been working on.

Energy efficiency is not glamorous and certainly not as heroic as nuclear power, but it is exceedingly effective. As Casten points out, the efficiency of our electrical grid has been the same since around 1960.

First things first, before the glamorous solutions, please—be they nuclear or solar.

George Mokray
Massachusetts, United States

Professor Rumelt has succeeded in sending the most important message: it's a new game out there, with new rules.

This is a good time for innovation, for simplifying interactions, and for creating new value pools. The costs must obviously be cut, but it is essential to use the opportunity to break through existing redundancies in the business structure. That is, reshaping costs now is much more important than only squeezing them out.

Every crisis is an opportunity, but it also encourages complacency and wishful thinking. Staying away from simple solutions will be, again, the real challenge.

Vihar Georgiev
Business Development Manager,
Cibola Energy, Bulgaria

From Our Online Discussions

Reader comments on our blog post about the centered-leadership model

A McKinsey survey showed how male and female executives from around the world think about and use the five dimensions of McKinsey's centered-leadership model: *meaning, managing energy, positive framing, connecting,* and *engaging.* **The model was introduced in the article "Centered leadership: How talented women thrive," from** *The McKinsey Quarterly,* **2008 Number 4.** *Quarterly* readers' discussion focused particularly on time management and on the interplay between work and personal life.

I think that time and energy are barriers to thinking (or excuses not to think) about what we love to do. The centered-leadership model resonated very strongly with me because it focuses our attention on us and, in a way, it shows that there is a way of combining it all together if we are able to find meaning, experience flow more often, and know what our goals are. Many times we are so engulfed in all the everyday requirements that come from both work and family that we rarely think about what we really love to do and whether we are experiencing this on day-to-day basis at work. I think that it is not possible to be a fulfilled person and a leader and a high achiever if one is not clear about one's passion in life.
—*Christina*

Five dimensions of leadership

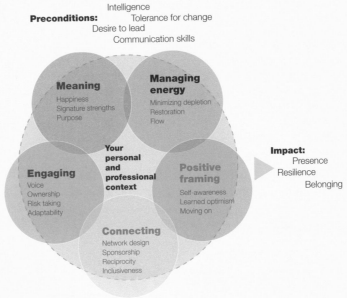

In general, culture relative to gender inside and outside organizations suggests it is likely for female maturation to occur faster and in a whole way (e.g., "centered"). I do think time and energy limits are barriers, sometimes, to focusing on other factors. The most progressive workplaces recognize working mothers need flexibility and that they still perform. Before too long, perhaps the same will be expected by working fathers. These issues are part of the reasons many of us drop out from corporate grinds and run our own enterprises with great success!

—*Lisa*

The ability to contribute in a meaningful way means that the right people are in the right positions, and irrespective of the "lines of demarcation" everyone has the opportunity to act—with the caveat that it be "on purpose" and focused on organizational goals and objectives. No organization will maximize its potential—led by women or men—if the compass is compromised. I don't think it is a gender thing.

—*Jackie*

I'm inclined to agree that the five dimensions are more about having a full life or being a well-rounded person, and are not a sufficient condition for great leadership. But they are probably necessary for good leadership.

—*Sophie*

As an executive coach, most of my clients are male senior executives. I find it fascinating that the five dimensions highlighted in this article are the very things that my clients want to work on. These are highly successful people, who want more than just hitting the numbers. It is gratifying to hear how they begin to enjoy their work more when they enjoy their lives more. Exploring their personal values and understanding the origins of those values helps them determine how to live deliberate lives. Perhaps because women must be aware of and clear about choices in their lives—professional and personal—they end up with the lives that bring them happiness as well as success. Or, maybe, they have a different definition of success.

—*Dawn Robertson*

In Brief

Research and perspectives on management

Promoting energy efficiency in the developing world **14**
Toolbox: Identifying employee skill gaps **18**
The Quarterly *Surveys* **19**
Conversation Starter: Mobilizing boards for change **20**
Speaking of Strategy: An interview with Alberto Alessi **22**
Management practices that drive supply chain success **24**

Promoting **energy efficiency** in the developing world

Diana Farrell and Jaana Remes

Big gains await developing countries if they raise their energy productivity, research by the McKinsey Global Institute (MGI) has found: they could slow the growth of their energy demand by more than half over the next 12 years—to 1.4 percent a year, from 3.4—which would leave demand some 25 percent lower in 2020 than it would otherwise have been (Exhibit 1). That is a reduction larger than total energy consumption in China today.

Policy makers and businesses in developing regions must not be deterred from boosting energy productivity (the output they achieve from the energy they consume) because of the present weakening economic environment and falling oil prices; these do not affect the long-term projections in the study.[1] Time is of the essence: developing economies will install half or more of the capital stock that will be in place in 2020 between now and then. Every building or industrial plant constructed without optimal energy efficiency represents a lost opportunity to lock in lower energy consumption for decades.

Just by using existing technologies that would pay for themselves in future energy savings, consumers and businesses could save some $600 billion a year by 2020. Companies that pioneer energy efficiency in their home markets will be well placed to carve out a leading position in the global market for "green" products and services before it matures. Indeed, 65 percent of available positive-return opportunities to boost energy productivity are located in developing regions (Exhibit 2).

The benefits of higher energy efficiency are achievable with an investment of $90 billion annually over the next 12 years— only about half of what these economies would otherwise need to spend on their energy supply infrastructure to keep pace with higher consumption. Indeed, because of lower labor costs, the price

tag for investing in energy productivity is on average 35 percent lower in developing economies than in advanced ones.

At present, a range of market failures and information barriers discourage developing countries from increasing their energy productivity, even with high energy prices. Capital constraints, particularly for low-income households, are a major hurdle. Consumers also tend to lack the information they need to make the right choices. Many companies, insulated from the true price of energy, have relatively little

EXHIBIT I

Higher energy productivity

End-use energy demand by region,[1] quadrillion British thermal units (QBTUs)

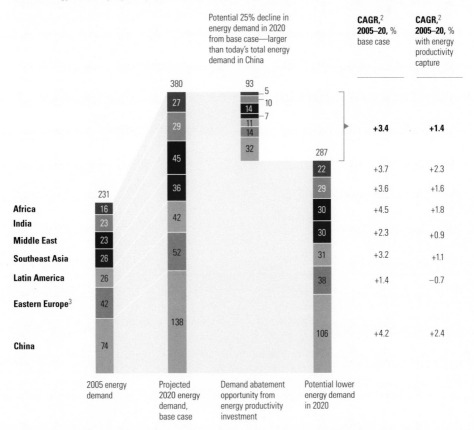

Potential 25% decline in energy demand in 2020 from base case—larger than today's total energy demand in China

	CAGR,[2] 2005–20, % base case	CAGR,[2] 2005–20, % with energy productivity capture
	+3.4	+1.4
	+3.7	+2.3
	+3.6	+1.6
Africa	+4.5	+1.8
Middle East	+2.3	+0.9
Southeast Asia	+3.2	+1.1
Latin America	+1.4	−0.7
China	+4.2	+2.4

2005 energy demand

Projected 2020 energy demand, base case

Demand abatement opportunity from energy productivity investment

Potential lower energy demand in 2020

[1] Figures may not sum to totals, because of rounding.
[2] Compound annual growth rate.
[3] Includes Belarus, Czech Republic, Estonia, Hungary, Latvia, Lithuania, Poland, Russia, and Slovakia.

Source: McKinsey Global Institute analysis

incentive to identify and invest in the fragmented energy savings opportunities that are available. And today's tighter credit markets are squeezing the financing of all investments—even less risky ones, such as those in energy efficiency.

MGI calculates that somewhat more than half of the current variation in energy productivity among developing countries can be explained by climate, industry structure, and energy policies (Exhibit 3). Climatic extremes that require the use of heating and cooling systems unavoidably increase energy consumption in relation to GDP in some regions. Heavy industrialization is a consideration because countries with large manufacturing sectors tend to consume more energy and have lower energy productivity. But for energy policy, there are adjustments that developing countries can make. MGI identifies four priority areas.

The first is to reduce energy subsidies, as they tend to lower energy productivity. The International Energy Agency (IEA) estimates that in 2005, these subsidies

totaled more than $250 billion a year in developing countries—more than the annual investment needed to build their electricity supply infrastructure. Protecting the poor from the stress of high energy prices is a legitimate goal. But there are other ways to achieve this and similar welfare goals at a lower cost. For example, in Latin America and elsewhere, governments have tried to reduce poverty by using conditional cash-transfer programs, which can also help compensate low-income households for high energy costs. To ease the transition to more efficient energy use, governments should consider providing finance for upgrades to more efficient equipment and use some of the savings from lower energy consumption to assist poor segments of the population.

Second, governments should provide incentives for utilities to improve energy efficiency and encourage their customers to do the same. Policy options include revenue incentives and certification programs that measure and reward progress toward achieving efficiency targets and also encourage the adoption of technologies,

EXHIBIT 2

Where the opportunities are

End-use energy demand abatement in 2020 by region,[1] %
100% = 143 quadrillion British thermal units (QBTUs)

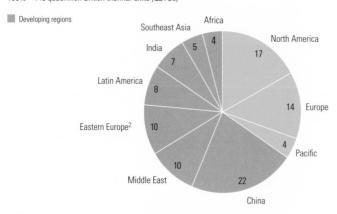

■ Developing regions

Africa
Southeast Asia
India 7
5
4
North America 17
Latin America 8
Europe 14
Eastern Europe[2] 10
Pacific 4
Middle East 10
22
China

[1]Figures do not sum to 100%, because of rounding.
[2]Includes Belarus, Czech Republic, Estonia, Hungary, Latvia, Lithuania, Poland, Russia, and Slovakia.

Source: McKinsey Global Institute analysis

EXHIBIT 3

Variation in energy productivity

Variation in energy productivity among developing countries,[1] 2005, %

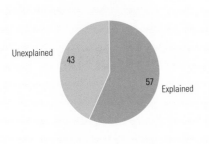

Unexplained 43

57 Explained

Type of contribution to variation in energy productivity,[2] %

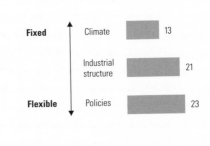

Fixed — Climate — 13

Industrial structure — 21

Flexible — Policies — 23

[1]Data covers 27 developing countries (defined as those with a 2007 average per capita income of less than $11,000, adjusted for purchasing-power parity).
[2]Climate is based on hot/cold days; industrial structure reflects the manufacturing and nonmanufacturing subsectors of the economy, combined with level of per capita income; policies include gas subsidies and gas taxes, as well as an index of corruption.

Source: Global Insight; International Energy Agency (IEA); national sources; McKinsey Global Institute analysis

such as smart metering, that help households better manage their energy use.

Implementing and enforcing energy efficiency standards is a third area for action. Such standards boost production of more efficient appliances and equipment and reduce their cost. Indonesia has recently adopted the UN technical regulation on auto energy efficiency, for example, and Ghana has pioneered standards for household appliances in Africa.

A fourth priority is encouraging public–private partnerships, such as collaborations between governments, energy service companies, utilities, and mortgage companies, to finance higher energy efficiency in buildings. China, which manufactures 70 percent of the world's lightbulbs, now has very large subsidies in place to promote the uptake of energy-efficient bulbs.

If developing countries and their businesses seize the initiative on energy productivity, they will cut their energy costs, insulate themselves from future energy shocks, and secure a more sustainable development path—benefits that are all the more desirable given the current global financial turmoil.

Diana Farrell is an alumnus of the McKinsey Global Institute, where **Jaana Remes** is a consultant.

[1] The study—conducted before the economic slowdown in late 2008—assumes, among other things, global GDP growth of 3.2 percent annually to 2020 (including, for example, 6.4 percent annual growth in China) and an average oil price of $50 a barrel. A fresh review of the data and underlying assumptions indicates that slowing worldwide economic growth in the near term will have minimal effects on the long-term projections in this article.

Toolbox

Identifying employee **skill gaps**

Oliver Triebel and Pierre Gurdjian

Many training programs don't yield the desired results. One reason is that they are usually launched without knowing where the gaps in employee skills exist. A good way to pinpoint these learning needs is to survey employees and let them evaluate the current skill levels of their peers and estimate the skill level their group must reach in order to be successful.

A manufacturing company that embarked on a major performance transformation chose to survey site leaders, middle managers, and frontline supervisors. Using a heat map to visualize the results, the company found, for instance, that while middle managers in one region needed training to improve several business competencies, those in another region had gaps in their leadership skills. Based on the results of the survey, the company realized it could save money and improve its chances of success by rolling out a program targeting the different competencies that each group needed to improve the most.

Illustrative example

■ More improvement required ■ Improvement required ■ Less improvement required

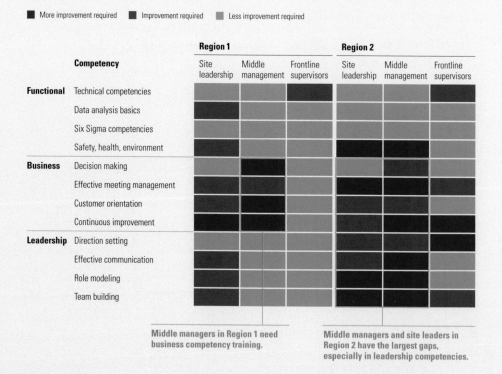

	Region 1			Region 2		
Competency	Site leadership	Middle management	Frontline supervisors	Site leadership	Middle management	Frontline supervisors
Functional Technical competencies						
Data analysis basics						
Six Sigma competencies						
Safety, health, environment						
Business Decision making						
Effective meeting management						
Customer orientation						
Continuous improvement						
Leadership Direction setting						
Effective communication						
Role modeling						
Team building						

Middle managers in Region 1 need business competency training.

Middle managers and site leaders in Region 2 have the largest gaps, especially in leadership competencies.

Oliver Triebel is an associate principal in McKinsey's Berlin office, and **Pierre Gurdjian** is a director in the Brussels office.

The Quarterly *Surveys*

Selected results from surveys of the *Quarterly*'s panel of global executives

Measuring **innovation**

% of respondents,[1] n = 1,075

■ Pursues
■ Formally assesses

What types of innovations does your organization pursue?

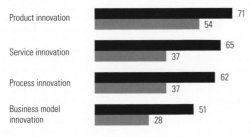

Product innovation — 71 / 54

Service innovation — 65 / 37

Process innovation — 62 / 37

Business model innovation — 51 / 28

[1]Respondents who answered "other" are not shown.

No matter what form of innovation companies pursue, far fewer measure it than pursue it. Those that do employ metrics are much likelier to measure outputs, such as customer satisfaction, than inputs, such as ideas in the pipeline. That could be a mistake. Companies reporting the highest contribution to growth from their innovation projects tend to be more interested in pursuing and measuring their innovations as a portfolio and therefore use metrics across the whole innovation process.

From "Assessing innovation metrics: McKinsey Global Survey Results," November 2008, which includes the responses of 1,075 executives from around the world.

Understanding what your **competitors might do**

% of respondents,[1] n = 1,552

■ Extension of existing strategy

Which of the following statements best describes your business unit's largest strategic initiative in your most recent full fiscal year?[2]

The next logical step in our existing strategic direction — 33

Increased investment in our existing strategy in our immediate market segment — 29

A completely new strategy — 15

Decreased investment in our existing strategy without a change in direction — 12

No new strategic initiatives in our business unit — 8

[1]Respondents who answered "other" or "don't know" are not shown.
[2]Strategic initiative defined as major change in direction or focus; excludes any decisions made in response to current global economic turmoil.

Companies have a good chance of anticipating their competitors' strategic moves. Indeed, only 15 percent of executives say their companies' largest initiative in the past year was a completely new strategy. Moreover, only 29 percent say their companies actively searched for a new strategy in the past five years, rather than simply responding to a challenge or opportunity—most of which would be equally visible to their competitors.

From "How companies can understand competitors' moves: McKinsey Global Survey Results," January 2009, which includes the responses of 1,552 executives from around the world.

Conversation Starter

**Short essays by leading thinkers
on management topics**

The crisis:
Mobilizing boards for change

Andrew Campbell and Stuart Sinclair

As companies grapple with uncertainty of a magnitude that few have experienced before, their boards should begin by questioning fundamental strategic assumptions: Is our view of the market realistic? Does our financing strategy take into account the new conditions? Do we need to change our incentive scheme? How can we come out stronger than our competitors?

Unfortunately, most corporate directors are likely to assume that radical change is unnecessary and that "normal service" will soon resume. Their experiences during less severe crises—such as those in 1990, 1997, or 2001—will lull them into a false sense of complacency; few will adjust their strategies and policies sufficiently. This behavior is the result of a clinically observed human trait of being overly influenced by past experiences and judgments. Experts on decision making call it *anchoring*. The problem is made worse by the natural rhythms that characterize how many boards are used to working—rhythms that tend to reinforce rather than challenge anchored thinking. We therefore argue that board chairmen need to play a special role in the coming months by challenging their boards to think things through afresh.

This is not an easy task. Board procedures are anchored too. Meetings, agendas, and timetables typically follow a preset annual pattern. Attempts to make changes are often resisted—in part because of habit and in part because those involved have busy calendars. Even if there is energy for fresh, substantive work, the diary may defeat the best intentions. Mobilizing the board to tackle the economic crisis requires a fundamental overhaul of how its members interact. The chairman needs to underline the gravity and urgency of the situation by summoning the board to extraordinary "credit crunch" meetings, "survival" meetings, "does our plan still make sense" meetings, and "how can we turn this pain into an opportunity" meetings. Without disrupting the rhythm, anchored thinking will continue to dominate.

The style of interaction can be another obstacle. Boards tend to establish patterns of behavior; for example, seating can become regularized, and some members may be expected to say little. Moreover, most boards have a default operating mode. Some place a premium on running smoothly—no disagreements, no late papers, no fluffed presentations, and no late finishes. Some are preoccupied with the formal aspects of governance: process dominates and content gets less attention. Some are financially oriented, with board members peering at their responsibilities through the numbers. But amidst all this

Successful CEOs will be those who can inspire constructive conflict and have the skill to manage such a dynamic environment. Unfortunately, there is a dearth of this kind of leadership talent in the American business world today.
—Jody Bicking

The solution is not only "to explicitly change the way the board interacts" but also to invite more women to serve on corporate boards. That will certainly shake up the status quo.
—Carol Frohlinger

You have to force people to voice their objections and help them to understand that opposing opinions do not paint you as a non-team player.
—Rudy Allen

heterogeneity lies, in our experience, one simple theme—there tends to be relatively little scope for genuine free thinking or for any fundamental reexamination of the premise of the company.

The solution is to explicitly change the way the board interacts. The chairman should insist that members articulate what they have thought but have not had the confidence to express. These conversations will often be more conceptual than rote and participants will have to take the risk of "saying something stupid." Chairmen will need to muster up the courage to take their boards into deep and frightening waters. Long-cherished assumptions, existing plans, or defined ambitions may be questioned.

Many boards use outsiders either to facilitate a change in style or to challenge the thinking of their members. In one board, the work involved identifying the six to ten premises of the company's plan for 2009. The outsider then interviewed each director and asked them to offer their opinions on each premise confidentially. When shown to the group, the results demonstrated that most of the board no longer believed the premises were valid. Letting go of past anchors may also require new, visceral experiences that trigger new thinking. This may mean encouraging directors to spend time with bankers,

visit customers or distributors or talk with middle managers. These new conversations will help directors feel the changes that are happening rather than just intellectualize them.

An additional job for the chairman is to ensure stronger follow-through than is normal: fresh thinking needs to lead to changes in plans and budgets. One board we know has followed up new thinking with weekly calls to confirm the new direction. Without dramatic leadership from chairmen, many companies will wander into 2009 hoping that their past view of the world will be restored— leaving them badly positioned to respond to the new environment.

Andrew Campbell is a director of the London-based Ashridge Strategic Management Centre and has written more than ten books based on his research. The latest, *Think Again–Why Good Leaders Make Bad Decisions and How to Keep It From Happening to You*, is coauthored with Sydney Finkelstein and Jo Whitehead (Harvard Business Press, 2009).

Stuart Sinclair is chairman and nonexecutive director of several companies in the United Kingdom and Eastern Europe and was previously the CEO of Tesco Personal Finance and GE Capital China. The opinions he expresses here are purely his own.

Speaking of Strategy

An interview with
Alberto Alessi

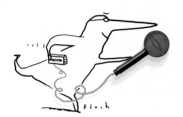

Marla M. Capozzi

Alberto Alessi is the third generation to lead his family's iconic design firm. In Alessi's view, both the ownership structure and the location of his company (about an hour north of Milan, Italy) have imbued it with a strong tradition of artisanship—and given its designers the freedom to create as they see fit. Here, Alessi discusses how he assesses an innovation's potential.

The *Quarterly*: *How do you assess the potential of product innovations?*

Alessi: We have a very helpful tool that we call, ironically, "the formula." It's a mathematical model that we use once we have a well-done prototype. Not the first or the second prototype, but from the third one on. The purpose of the formula is to understand what the reaction of our final customers could be toward this new product and what the product's life could be should we decide to start production.

The *Quarterly*: *How did you develop "the formula"?*

Alessi: It all started in the beginning of the '90s, when my brothers were curious why I was doing certain projects and not other projects. And of course, I didn't know. Because everything was happening in my stomach. But it was a good question. So I started thinking how to answer. And what I did was put together all the 300 projects I had developed during my career until then.

These 300 projects had very different lives. Some were big successes. Some a bit more than that. Some were big fiascos. And the rest were in the range of a little bit better, a little bit worse. I was, of course, convinced there was a reason for these outcomes.

When I tried to explore the reasons for each product's life, I came out with four parameters. All four were equally important for the final customer, but only two were central parameters for Alessi; the other two were peripheral for us.

The first central parameter is the degree to which people say, "Oh, what a beautiful object," which represents the creation of a relationship between the object and the individual. We call this SMI, which stands for sensation, memory, imagination. The second is the use that people can make of an object in order to communicate with other people. By this I mean that objects have become the main channel through which we convey our values, status, and personality to others—fashion is a typical case in point. Objects can have status value or style value. By way of example, a gold Rolex watch is a status symbol, which suggests economic wealth, whereas a style symbol may be exemplified by an Aldo Rossi teapot, which reveals cultural sensitivity and familiarity with the architectural domain. Jean Baudrillard, a French sociologist, brilliantly expounded concepts like these.

The peripheral parameters are function and price. Each of these parameters has five degrees.

Visit mckinseyquarterly.com for the full interview and an interactive video featuring Alberto Alessi.

'It makes no sense for me to reduce risk; we use the formula so we can afford more risk'

Alberto Alessi
Corporate general manager
Alessi

1990
Juicer by
Philippe Stark

The Alessi formula

Function	Sensation, Memory, Imagination	Communication & Language	Price	
Practical Functional Easy to use Easy to clean Helpful	Pleasant to senses Memorable Evocative Creatively satisfying	Status Stylish Trendy Curtural Self-Expressive	Comparable Expresses true value Related to quality	
Perverse	Unpleasant	Out	Too Expensive	1
Questionable	Not very nice	Doubtful	Expensive	2
Standard	Neutral	Acceptable	In line	3
Functional	Attractive	In	Profitable	4
Brilliant	Exciting	Illuminating	I'll take two!	5

1988
Coffee maker by
Aldo Rossi

The formula doesn't work for everything. But when we have a long history with a product, it works perfectly. If I have to evaluate a pot or a coffee maker or a kettle, for example, the score indicates exactly the number of pieces that we can sell.

When we are exploring a new area—for example, when we were designing a pen, which was completely new terrain for Alessi—then it becomes more difficult. The formula needs to be tuned in a different way. But the principle is the same.

Fundamentally, we use the formula so we can afford more risk. I don't want to reduce the risk. Given my business, it makes no sense for me to reduce risk. I just need to determine where I am in order to have the opportunity to take a bit more risk.

This interview was conducted by **Marla Capozzi,** an associate principal in McKinsey's Boston office.

Management practices that drive
supply chain success

Bruce Constantine, Brian D. Ruwadi, and Joshua Wine

Companies with high-performing supply chains differentiate themselves from ordinary performers through the superior application of six management practices. As a result, these companies enjoy lower distribution and logistics costs, better service outcomes, and better inventory performance than others do. Against a backdrop of economic uncertainty and rising supply chain risk, our findings have implications for high-tech, manufacturing, packaged-goods, pharmaceutical, and retailing companies.

To study the link between supply chain performance and the underlying practices driving it, we conducted in-depth interviews with operations executives at 60 companies across Europe and North America. The research, conducted together with the Georgia Institute of Technology's College of Management, assessed the performance of the respondents' companies in more than 50 aspects of supply chain management, including business processes, corporate culture, network configurations, organizational structures, strategy, supporting infrastructure, and the capabilities of personnel. After interviewers plotted the executives' responses on a scale of one to five (five was the highest), the results were organized into tertiles and compared with supply chain performance metrics provided by the respondents on cost, inventory, and service levels.

When we examined the relationship between the scores and performance, six broad practices emerged as significant (Exhibit 1). While no company we studied had mastered all six, organizations displaying strength across them appear

to outperform competitors in service (the timeliness and completeness of customer deliveries), inventory (the ratio of inventory levels to cost of goods sold), and distribution and logistics costs (Exhibit 2). That finding belies the notion that trade-offs are inevitable in these areas.

To manage complexity, for instance, 50 percent of our top service performers use segmentation techniques to create distinct supply chains (in their broader supply networks) to serve different customer groups with unique products. Only 29 percent of average companies do. Notably, top companies take this approach without increasing their supply chain costs relative to average companies. Likewise, two-thirds of top companies consider supply chain design processes and product- and portfolio-development processes concurrently, versus half of average companies. Leaders also regularly examine product portfolios to eliminate complexity that doesn't add value.

The case for developing best-practice segmentation skills is compelling. Organizations scoring among the top one-third of survey participants on this dimension are 2.5 times as likely to be leaders in inventory performance and twice as likely to be leaders in service as companies in the bottom third.

Top companies also excel in optimizing end-to-end efficiency. Ordinary companies apply cost reduction techniques within individual functions (such as transportation), but top ones apply lean-management tools throughout the supply chain. The companies with the lowest supply chain costs are also more likely to entrust managers with

EXHIBIT 1

Practices that matter

⊘ No significant advantage or disadvantage

Supply-chain-management practices	Improved likelihood of being top-third performer vs bottom-third performer[1]		
	Service	Cost	Inventory
1 Link supply chain strategy to company strategy; set clear aspirations. • Supply chain group is key stakeholder in business-planning decisions. • Corporate strategy translated into tangible supply chain targets and initiatives.	1.9x	1.3x	1.4x
2 Segment the supply chain to master the product and service complexity that matters most. • Organization manages the portfolio to eliminate complexity that does not add value. • Discrete material and information flows are used to manage different products and customers most efficiently.	2.0x	⊘	2.5x
3 Tailor supply network to optimize service, cost, and risk goals. • Company selectively invests in flexibility over efficiency where required. • Customer service requirements considered in supply network decisions.	1.8x	⊘	2.3x
4 Use lean tools to optimize supply chain from end to end. • Supply chain managers own end-to-end costs to ensure optimization efforts don't improve one function's performance at expense of another's.	⊘	1.3x	2.0x
5 Create integrated/robust sales- and operations-planning (S&OP) processes. • Sales, finance, supply chain teams actively collaborate in planning activities. • Planning teams across the organization execute processes with discipline.	1.3x	2.6x	4.0x
6 Find top talent; hold people accountable. • Supply chain experts have deep functional expertise, general business skills. • Customized formal training programs are used to fill capability gaps. • Strong culture of accountability is cultivated.	1.7x	⊘	1.6x
General likelihood across all 6 practices (ratio of relative probabilities)	1.4x	1.7x	2.7x

[1] Figures are not additive; top performance is defined as follows: service—top one-third among respondents on timeliness and completeness of customer deliveries; cost—top one-third among respondents on distribution and logistics costs; inventory—top one-third among respondents on ratio of inventory levels to cost of goods sold.

Source: McKinsey in conjunction with Georgia Institute of Technology's College of Management

end-to-end control over them, thus increasing the likelihood that management decisions will improve the whole business and not just certain functions. These companies are also nearly three times more likely than the others to share both information (say, about customer demand) and improvement metrics across functions.

Top performers take a methodical approach to demand and production planning, as well. Using cross-functional teams empowered to make decisions ranging from revising inventory safety stocks to reallocating products to manage shortages, these companies tightly integrate forecasting, supply planning, and production-scheduling processes. They rigorously forecast performance across multiple dimensions—for instance, by customer group, or distribution channel. They are twice as likely as ordinary companies to use planning and performance information to adjust inventory levels and storage locations dynamically in order to minimize inventory holding costs without compromising quality of service, among other purposes. One executive commented, "We turned the corner when we started rewarding disciplined decision making rather than heroic acts made in the name of customer service." The results? Companies scoring among the top one-third

EXHIBIT 2

Gaining the advantage

Companies that excel at the 6 most important practices...

Average survey score (1–5 scale) across the most important practices

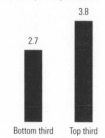

Bottom third — 2.7
Top third — 3.8

... are much more likely to be top service, cost, and inventory performers that create a real advantage over other companies.

Improved likelihood of being a top performer vs a bottom performer

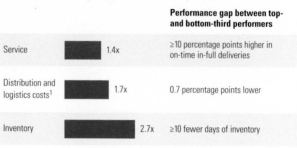

	Improved likelihood	Performance gap between top- and bottom-third performers
Service	1.4x	≥10 percentage points higher in on-time in-full deliveries
Distribution and logistics costs[1]	1.7x	0.7 percentage points lower
Inventory	2.7x	≥10 fewer days of inventory

[1] Absolute difference in distribution and logistics cost as percentage of sales.

Source: McKinsey in conjunction with Georgia Institute of Technology's College of Management

of survey respondents in this area are 4.0 times more likely than low performers to be inventory leaders, 2.6 times more likely to be cost leaders, and 1.3 times more likely to perform strongly on service.

Top companies achieve the discipline required to excel in these areas partly by improving the skills of their employees. Talent leaders are more likely than others to use functional rotation and to groom supply chain leaders through formal capability-building programs. Such programs help companies to increase the competency and awareness of leaders across the business on supply chain issues, while also ensuring that consistent approaches are used—and constantly improved—over time.

What practices don't appear to be important? Notably, investments in formal IT systems (beyond basic enterprise-resource-planning ones) don't appear to improve supply chain performance as much as some managers expect. Companies relying more on spreadsheets and other informal solutions were nearly twice as likely to be cost leaders—and nearly three times as likely to be inventory leaders—as companies using formal IT systems extensively. That finding supports our view that they cannot replace strong processes, capabilities, and decision making. As one executive put it, "Our systems cannot be smarter than our colleagues, or we will have problems."

Our research also identified important interdependencies between practices: in particular, two of the six we studied require strong performance in other practices. Companies seeking a road map for improving the efficiency and performance of their supply chains may therefore well have different natural starting points.

Bruce Constantine is a consultant in McKinsey's Boston office, **Brian Ruwadi** is a principal in the Cleveland office, and **Josh Wine** is an associate principal in the Tel Aviv office.

We welcome your comments on these articles.
Please send them to quarterly_comments@mckinsey.com.

On the cover:

What to do about health care

28
Why Americans pay more
for health care

40
Three imperatives for
improving US health care

54
Improving Japan's health
care system

Artwork by Brian Stauffer

Why Americans pay more for health care

The United States spends more on health care than comparable countries do and more than its wealth would suggest. Here's how—and why.

Diana Farrell, Eric S. Jensen, and Bob Kocher

The health care debate in the United States excites great passion. Issues such as how to make care available, to structure insurance, and to rein in spending by the government, corporations, and individuals frequently take center stage. Often missing, though, are basic economic facts. New research from the McKinsey Global Institute (MGI) and McKinsey's health care practice sheds light on a critical piece of the puzzle: the cost of care.

Our research indicates that the United States spends $650 billion more on health care than might be expected given the country's wealth and the experience of comparable members of the Organisation for Economic Co-operation and Development (OECD). The research also pinpoints where that extra spending goes. Roughly two-thirds of it pays for outpatient care, including visits to physicians, same-day hospital treatment, and emergency-room care. The next-largest contributors to the extra spending are drugs and administration and insurance.

Diana Farrell is an alumnus of the McKinsey Global Institute; **Bob Kocher** is an alumnus of McKinsey's Washington, DC, office, where **Eric Jensen** is a consultant.

It's not clear whether the United States gets $650 billion worth of extra value. Parts of the US health care system, such as its best hospitals, are clearly world class. Cutting-edge drugs and treatments are available earlier there, and waiting times to see physicians tend to be lower. Yet the country lags behind other OECD members on a number of outcome measures, including life expectancy and infant mortality. Furthermore,

access to health care is unequal: more than 45 million Americans lack insurance.

The challenge for health care reformers is to retain the current system's strengths while addressing its deficiencies and curbing costs. That won't be easy. Our research on the system's costs and the incentives underlying them indicates that without the involvement of all major stakeholders (such as hospitals, payers, and doctors) reform is likely to prove elusive. The research also suggests that while there are many possible paths to reform, it is unlikely to succeed unless it deals comprehensively with health care demand, supply, and payments.

A $650 billion spending gap

Across the world, richer countries generally spend a disproportionate share of their income on health care. In the language of economics, it is a "superior good." Just as wealthier people might spend a larger proportion of their income to buy bigger homes or homes in better neighborhoods, wealthier countries tend to spend more on health care.

Yet even accounting for this economic relationship, the United States still spends $650 billion more on health care than might be inferred from its wealth. MGI arrived at this figure by using data from 13 OECD countries to develop a metric called estimated spending according to wealth (ESAW), which adjusts health care expenditures according to per capita GDP. No other developed country's spending above the ESAW level approaches that of the United States (Exhibit 1).

EXHIBIT 1

More than expected

Trendline of countries' expected spending according to wealth, 2006

Health care spending per capita,[1] $

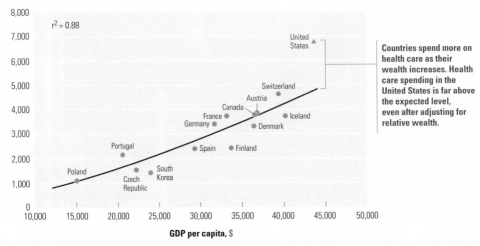

Countries spend more on health care as their wealth increases. Health care spending in the United States is far above the expected level, even after adjusting for relative wealth.

r^2 is the proportion of variance explained by a regression.
[1] Adjusted for purchasing-power parity.

Source: Organisation for Economic Co-operation and Development (OECD)

Is it paying so much more because its people are less healthy than those of other countries? Our research indicates that the answer is no. While lifestyle-induced diseases, such as obesity, are on the rise in the United States, the most common diseases are, on average, slightly less prevalent there than in peer OECD members. The factors contributing to the lower disease rates include the relatively younger (and therefore less disease-prone) population of the United States, as well as the low prevalence of smoking-related problems. Factoring in the average cost of treatment for each disease, we still find that the relative health of the US population does not account for the higher cost of health care.

Analyzing the problem

MGI broke down health care costs into their components to identify the sources of this higher-than-expected spending (Exhibit 2). Outpatient care is by far the largest and fastest-growing part of it, accounting for more than $400 billion, or two-thirds of the $650 billion figure. The cost of drugs and the cost of health care administration and insurance (all nonmedical costs incurred by health care payers) account for an additional $98 billion and $91 billion, respectively, in extra spending. By contrast, US expenditures on long-term and home care, as well as on durable medical equipment (such as eyeglasses, wheelchairs, and hearing aids), is actually less than would be expected given the country's wealth.

EXHIBIT 2

High outpatient costs

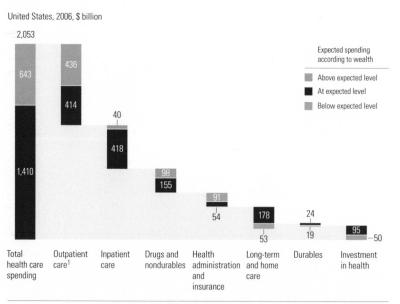

United States, 2006, $ billion

Expected spending according to wealth
- Above expected level
- At expected level
- Below expected level

Total health care spending / Outpatient care[1] / Inpatient care / Drugs and nondurables / Health administration and insurance / Long-term and home care / Durables / Investment in health

[1]Outpatient care includes care in the offices of physicians and dentists, same-day visits to hospitals (including emergency departments), ambulatory surgery, diagnostic-imaging centers, and other same-day care facilities.

Source: Organisation for Economic Co-operation and Development (OECD); McKinsey Global Institute analysis

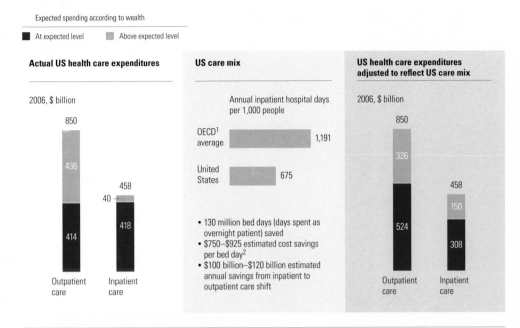

EXHIBIT 3

Still costly

Expected spending according to wealth

■ At expected level   ▨ Above expected level

Actual US health care expenditures

2006, $ billion

850

436

40

458

418

414

Outpatient care   Inpatient care

US care mix

Annual inpatient hospital days per 1,000 people

OECD[1] average: 1,191

United States: 675

• 130 million bed days (days spent as overnight patient) saved
• $750–$925 estimated cost savings per bed day[2]
• $100 billion–$120 billion estimated annual savings from inpatient to outpatient care shift

US health care expenditures adjusted to reflect US care mix

2006, $ billion

850

326

524

458

150

308

Outpatient care   Inpatient care

[1] Organisation for Economic Co-operation and Development.
[2] Estimated variable costs of lower-acuity care shifted into an outpatient setting.

Source: OECD; McKinsey Global Institute analysis

Outpatient care

The high and fast-growing cost of outpatient care reflects a structural shift in the United States away from inpatient settings, such as overnight hospital stays. Today, the US system delivers 65 percent of all care in outpatient contexts, up from 43 percent in 1980, and well above the OECD average of 52 percent. In theory, this shift should help to save money, since fixed costs in outpatient settings tend to be lower than the cost of overnight hospital stays. In reality, however, the shift to outpatient care has added to—not taken away from—total system costs because of the higher utilization of outpatient care in the United States.

We evaluated the economic impact of this structural shift by analyzing US inpatient care and comparing it with the practices of other OECD health systems. We estimate that the United States saves $100 billion to $120 billion a year on inpatient care thanks to shorter hospital stays and fewer hospital admissions. If we attribute these savings to the US health system's ability to provide care in outpatient settings, that would reduce above-ESAW outpatient expenditures—but only to $326 billion. This enormous figure still represents half of the US health care system's $650 billion in extra costs (Exhibit 3).

The two largest and fastest-growing categories of outpatient spending are same-day hospital care and visits to physicians' offices (Exhibit 4).

EXHIBIT 4

The doctor is in

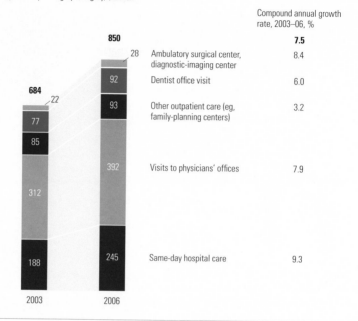

US outpatient spending by category, $ billion

Compound annual growth rate, 2003–06, %

850		**7.5**
28	Ambulatory surgical center, diagnostic-imaging center	8.4
92	Dentist office visit	6.0
93	Other outpatient care (eg, family-planning centers)	3.2
392	Visits to physicians' offices	7.9
245	Same-day hospital care	9.3

684
22
77
85
312
188

2003   2006

Source: Analysts' reports; Medical Expenditure Panel Survey (MEPS), US Census Bureau; Organisation for Economic Co-operation and Development (OECD); US Department of Health and Human Services; US Medicare Payment Advisory Commission (MedPAC)

From 2003 to 2006, the cost of these two categories increased by 9.3 and 7.9 percent a year, respectively. Growth in the number of visits played only a modest role in explaining the increase in costs—the number of same-day hospital visits rose by 2.1 percent annually, and the number of visits to physicians' offices remained relatively flat during this period.

Far more important was a surge in the average cost per visit resulting from factors such as the additional care delivered during visits, a shift toward more expensive procedures (for example, diagnostic ones such as CT and MRI scans), and absolute price increases for equivalent procedures.[1] In all likelihood, costs have also gone up because over the past decade there has been a marked shift in the delivery of care, from general practitioners to specialists.

Behind those proximate causes, several forces contribute to the rising cost of outpatient care across the entire range of settings, not just same-day hospital stays and visits to physicians' offices. For starters,

[1] CT (computerized tomography) and MRI (magnetic resonance imaging) scans are diagnostic tests that provide high-resolution pictures of the structure of any organ or part of the body requiring examination.

outpatient care is highly profitable—US hospitals earn a significant percentage of their profits from elective same-day care—which prompts investments in the facilities and people supporting it. These investments can be recouped only by offering more (and more expensive) services. The significant degree of discretion that physicians have over the course and extent of outpatient treatment also probably plays a role, as does the fee-for-service reimbursement system, which creates financial incentives to provide more outpatient care.

Finally, there is no effective check on it. On average, the out-of-pocket expense of patients represents only 15 percent of the total cost, so they are relatively insensitive to it and apt to follow the advice of their physicians. Other countries also have low out-of-pocket expenses but use supply-oriented controls to compensate for the lack of demand-side value consciousness.

Pharmaceuticals

After outpatient care, the category with the highest above-ESAW expenditures, at $98 billion, is prescription drugs—not because Americans are buying more of them but rather because they cost 50 percent more than equivalent products in other OECD countries (Exhibit 5).[2] The United States also uses a more expensive mix of drugs; the price of a

[2] Fifty percent represents the weighted average premium for branded drugs (77 percent), biologics (35 percent), and generics (−11 percent).

EXHIBIT 5

A high premium

$ per pill; index: average price for 5 EU countries[1] = 100

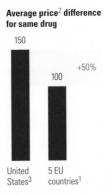

Average price[2] difference for same drug

For comparable drugs, US prices are 50 percent higher than those in other developed countries . . .

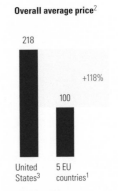

Overall average price[2]

. . . and the use of a more expensive mix of drugs in the United States increases average prices even more.

[1] France, Germany, Italy, Spain, and United Kingdom.
[2] Assumes 15% rebates from manufacturers to payers and pharmacy benefit managers.
[3] Manufacturer price.

Source: IMS Health; McKinsey Global Institute analysis

statistically average pill is 118 percent higher than that of its OECD equivalents. One reason is probably that new drugs, which tend to carry a price premium, are widely prescribed one to two years earlier in the United States than in Europe.

Several frequent explanations for higher US drug prices deserve examination. One is the wealth of the United States, which enables it to spend more on economically superior goods, such as drugs. Another is that high US prices subsidize research and development for the rest of the world. Marketing and sales spending by companies is higher in the United States than in other OECD countries (which generally restrict direct-to-physician or consumer advertising), and that also could play a role.

But none of these factors, by itself, can explain the gap between the price of drugs in the United States and the rest of the OECD. When we adjust for US wealth, we find that the country's branded-drug prices should carry a premium of some 30 percent, not 77 percent for branded small-molecule drugs. Similarly, if global pharma R&D spending—$40 billion to $50 billion in 2006—were financed entirely through higher branded-drug prices, the US price premium over similar countries would be 23 to 28 percent. Finally, in 2006 the sales and marketing expenditures of US pharma companies came to $30 billion to $40 billion, only 17 to 23 percent of current US prices.

*The United States can take **no single path** to address the level and growth of every one of its health care costs*

Health administration and insurance

The third-largest source of above-ESAW spending is health administration and insurance, at $91 billion. In this category, the United States spent $486 per capita in 2006—twice the outlay of the next-highest spender, France, with $248, and nearly five times the average of $103 across peer OECD countries.

Of the $91 billion in above-expected spending, $63 billion is attributable to private payers. Profits and taxes—a negligible expense in OECD countries with single-payer systems—account for nearly half of this total. The cost of public administration for Medicare, Medicaid, and other government programs accounts for the remaining $28 billion in US above-ESAW spending.

These higher costs largely reflect the diversity and number of payers as well as the multistate regulation of the US health care system. Its structure creates additional costs and inefficiencies: redundant

EXHIBIT 6

An added burden

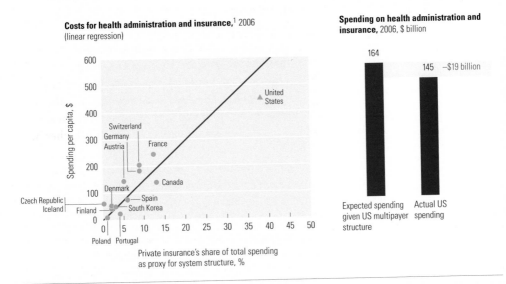

Costs for health administration and insurance,[1] 2006
(linear regression)

Spending on health administration and insurance, 2006, $ billion

[Left scatter plot: Spending per capita, $ (vertical axis 0 to 600) vs. Private insurance's share of total spending as proxy for system structure, % (horizontal axis 0 to 50). Labeled points include United States, Switzerland, Germany, Austria, France, Canada, Denmark, Spain, South Korea, Czech Republic, Iceland, Finland, Poland, Portugal.]

[Right bar chart: 164 (Expected spending given US multipayer structure), 145 (Actual US spending), −$19 billion]

[1] Adjusted for purchasing-power parity.

Source: Organisation for Economic Co-operation and Development (OECD); McKinsey Global Institute analysis

marketing, underwriting, claims processing, and management overhead. In other OECD countries, with less-fragmented payment systems, these costs are much lower. Interestingly, we find that given the structure of the US system, its administrative costs are actually $19 billion less than expected, suggesting that payers have had some success in restraining costs (Exhibit 6).

Of course, the US multipayer system could create value to the extent that it develops effective programs to promote health and prevent disease, competes to drive down prices, innovates to improve customer service or benefits, or offers patients greater choice. But do the virtues of the US system outweigh its inefficiencies, and can these inefficiencies be reduced within its current structure?

A framework for reform

The United States can take no single path to address the level and growth of every one of its health care costs. Any reform effort should involve all of the system's stakeholders, for the inclusion of hospitals, payers, and doctors in the reform effort will increase the odds of arriving at a plan for change that each party will truly embrace. Furthermore, each party can play a distinct role in addressing the full spectrum of issues that must be part of any major system overhaul. For each of these areas, there are several possibilities for reform—such as raising public awareness, creating appropriate incentives, mandating desired behavior, and taking direct action.

For health care reform to generate lasting improvements in cost, quality, access, and equity, it must effectively address supply, demand, and payment.[3] A number of our McKinsey colleagues recently completed an effort to determine what would be required to change trends in health care costs fundamentally. Here, we briefly lay out the principal issues for consideration by all health care reformers.

Demand

The general health of the US population is a significant issue. Although disease is no more prevalent in the United States than in peer OECD countries, the health of its population is falling, and this decline contributes to the growth in medical costs. In fact, our analysis suggests that in the two-year period from 2003 to 2005, the decline raised them by $20 billion to $40 billion. Reformers should therefore focus on the preventative efforts that present the largest opportunity to improve overall health and thereby save money.

Related articles on mckinseyquarterly.com

Transforming US hospitals

Value creation in health care: A sector-by-sector analysis

What consumers want in health care

Equally important is the lack of any real value consciousness. In the United States, the "average" consumer of health care pays for only 12 percent of its total cost directly out of pocket (down from 47 percent in 1960), as well as for 25 percent of health care insurance premiums, a share that has stayed relatively constant for the last decade. Well-insured patients who bear little, if any, of the cost of their treatment have no incentive to be value-conscious health care consumers.

Moreover, even if they wanted to be value conscious, they don't know enough. Despite recent efforts to expand consumer access to information on health care, its cost and quality remain opaque—arguably more so than in any other consumer industry. Consumers also know vastly less than providers do and therefore understandably rely on the advice and guidance of physicians. If Americans are to become more value-conscious consumers of health care, reformers must therefore determine how to create an appropriate level of price sensitivity and to give patients the right information, decision tools, and incentives.

[3] For more on a reform framework encompassing supply, demand, and payment for care, see Diana Farrell, Nicolaus P. Henke, and Paul D. Mango, "Universal principles for health care reform," mckinseyquarterly.com, February 2007; and Jean P. Drouin, Viktor Hediger, and Nicolaus Henke, "Health care costs: A market-based view," mckinseyquarterly.com, September 2008.

Supply

In many industries, such as consumer electronics, innovation tends to drive down prices. The opposite is true in health care, where lower prices don't necessarily boost sales and may even create the perception of low quality. Instead, innovation tends to focus on the development of increasingly more expensive products and techniques. High-priced technologies, from imaging to surgical equipment, also mean higher reimbursements for providers, who therefore demand cutting-edge products. So what emerges is a constant cycle of cost inflation along the entire health care value chain—from manufacturers of health products to equipment manufacturers to physicians to hospitals to payers and, ultimately, to employers and patients. At each step, the stakeholders absorb part of the cost increase and attempt to pass an even larger one onto the next stakeholder. Reformers must determine how to address this cost inflation cycle while retaining the beneficial aspects of innovation.

Intermediation

Medicare and many commercial payers base their reimbursements for inpatient care on episodes or diagnosis-related groups (DRGs). This forces providers to bear part of the risk of treating a patient and largely creates incentives to use resources efficiently. But fee-for-service reimbursement, the predominant method in outpatient treatment, does not have that effect and actually gives providers strong financial incentives to provide more (and more costly) care, not more value. Fear of malpractice suits boosts care volumes too. Our research indicates that the direct costs of malpractice are limited—about $30 billion in 2006—but the risk of litigation creates an incentive to err on the side of caution. Reformers therefore need to develop more effective financing and payment approaches ensuring that care providers have the right incentives to give patients an appropriate type and amount of care.

Medicare's role in influencing coverage and pricing dynamics also bears investigation. Private payers use this public program as a critical benchmark, more often than not following its lead, when they make decisions about which new procedures and technologies to reimburse. Because Medicare essentially uses a cost-plus formula to set reimbursement rates, it puts care providers under less pressure to reduce expenses than it could with another reimbursement mechanism. What's more, trends in the reimbursement rates of commercial payers are strongly correlated—but inversely—with Medicare pricing trends: private insurers grant providers higher increases when Medicare reimbursements grow more slowly. This suggests both that Medicare prices partly drive so-called market prices and that care providers have a significant amount of pricing power with private insurers. Reformers need to determine how public programs, such as Medicare and Medicaid, can lead the market toward rational change in reimbursement approaches and levels.

We welcome your
comments on this article.
Please send them to
quarterly_comments@
mckinsey.com.

Reform won't be easy. But armed with the facts about what the United States spends on different aspects of health care, how much above what might be expected that spending really is, and the underlying economic dynamics of the system, policy makers will have a better chance to curb the growth of costs. ✚

Letters to the Editor

Reader comments on "Why Americans pay more for health care" from mckinseyquarterly.com.

While very interesting, I feel your analysis leaves out a key detail: *why* are Americans using more complex treatments, and a greater number of these treatments? If you ask the physicians who prescribe these treatments, I think you'd find that a root cause is the rise in medical malpractice lawsuits. Doctors are prescribing more complex procedures (and a greater number of procedures) to protect themselves from litigation. This is an area that should be focused on when researching this topic for future publications.

Matt Hudnall
Connecticut, United States

Analysis in the paper shows that almost all the causes of higher-than-expected health care expenditures in the US are rooted in the behavior of providers, insurers, and pharmaceutical firms. And yet your recommended reforms concentrate on consumers. Strange indeed! The OECD countries with lower expenditures you cite have tight regulation of provider and insurer behavior and little or no competition. Why not recommend what is known to work elsewhere? It may be politically difficult to take on the providers, insurers, and big pharma, but as analysts we have a responsibility to speak truth to power.

M. Ramesh
The University of Hong Kong
Hong Kong

I am in a unique position as a consultant to both physicians (practice management) and employers (health plan management). I am privy to the financials of both industry sectors. Despite being initially surprised by your conclusions, my sense is that they are correct. I have seen a rise in employer health-plan expenses in recent years that is difficult to explain. At the same time, physicians are ever entrepreneurial—adding new services and technologies as payers attempt to push patients to outpatient settings through benefit plan design— and constitutional law protects most hospitals leading to absolute price increases.

The rise in the absolute cost of outpatient care in hospitals has not been well identified, though patient demand for specialty care physicians does result in much higher outpatient costs. Specialists perform more tests and tend to get compensated for them as they are generally members of large practices that own and operate their own ancillary services (such as diagnostic imaging and laboratory services) and facilities (such as ambulatory surgery centers). What you have now effectively proven is that unless patients pay more of the bill or are prevented from getting to specialists early and often, the drivers of higher outpatient costs cannot be prevented.

The delivery model of workplace-based clinics staffed by nurse practitioners needs to be expanded— to community health centers and public-health departments, among others—to get patients more primary care access and wellness and early intervention at less cost. And of course, patients who make poor lifestyle choices should pay more for health care. Unfortunately, these same individuals often have psychosocial issues that lead to continued poor lifestyle choices. Hence, the documented rise in mental and behavioral health diagnoses with Selective Serotonin Reuptake Inhibitor (SSRI) pharmaceutical prescriptions. Not an easy conundrum to solve.

Bob Blake
President, MedCapital Advisors, LLC
North Carolina, United States

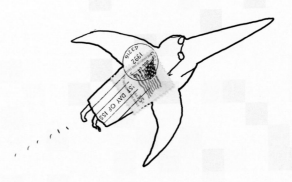

Visit mckinseyquarterly.com for more reader responses to this article.

Three imperatives for improving US health care

Making health care more affordable is the key to making the US system sustainable. We can bring three of the largest sources of underlying costs and their growth under control.

Paul D. Mango and Vivian E. Riefberg

Reforming the US health care system presents a daunting challenge, and there will be no shortage of proposals as the Obama administration prepares to handle it. Appropriately, the early dialogue has focused on extending coverage to the uninsured. However, any reform also needs to address the underlying problem—the relentless annual growth in the cost of health care—or reform will ultimately be inadequate. Poor affordability contributes directly to the unacceptably high number of uninsured Americans and presents a grave threat to the system's sustainability.

To stem these high and rising costs, the public and private sectors should cooperate to tackle three underlying problems, starting with the high incidence and cost of treating lifestyle- and behavior-induced diseases, such as obesity. These diseases are responsible not only for a majority of the deaths in the United States but also for the fastest-growing share of health care costs. Second, public and private stakeholders should make health care more affordable and improve its quality by minimizing the economic distortions that now tend to prevent consumers and providers from making value-conscious decisions. Finally, we need to simplify the system's pervasive and unnecessary administrative complexity to remove the waste that drives up costs, to facilitate the real-time flow of critical information, and to promote the introduction of productivity-enhancing technologies.

Paul Mango is a director in McKinsey's Pittsburgh office, and Vivian Riefberg is a director in the Washington, DC, office.

Regardless of the mechanism for administering or financing the system, we believe that without addressing these three issues, the sustainability of the system will be threatened. Solving the problems won't be easy. The weaknesses and considerable strengths of the modern US health care system are the products of an evolution that began nearly seven decades ago, and lasting change will surely take years to achieve. Nevertheless, by addressing the growth of costs and thus making the system more affordable, we can extend its benefits more quickly to larger numbers of people.

The state of the system

The US health care system is the world's largest. It is also by far the most expensive, consuming 16 percent of GDP. Research by the McKinsey Global Institute indicates that the United States spends about $650 billion a year more on health care than its wealth would suggest (see "Why Americans pay more for health care," in this issue).

Even more worrisome are the rapid increase in health care costs and the resulting rise in insurance premiums. Indeed, in recent years the growth of costs has outstripped the growth of both the country's GDP and of its workers' per capita income. The premiums of commercial health insurance policies, paid largely by employers, help subsidize health care for the uninsured and for people in government-sponsored programs (Exhibit 1). Since 1999, the cost of such a policy for a family of four has more than doubled. Today, it equals about one-quarter of the median US household income ($50,740).

EXHIBIT 1

A silent subsidy

Typical US regional hospital system, FY 2006–08, %

Distribution of hospital's net revenue[1]

100% = $900 million

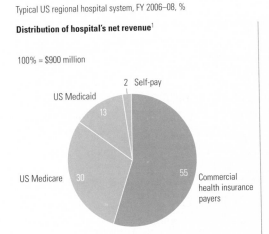

Hospital's profitability by type of insurance, EBITDA[2] margin

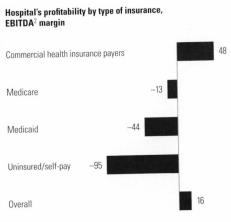

Commercial health insurance payers	48
Medicare	−13
Medicaid	−44
Uninsured/self-pay	−95
Overall	16

[1]Gross charges net of contractual allowances/adjustments and bad debt.
[2]Earnings before interest, taxes, depreciation, and amortization.

Source: Various statistics from representative US hospital; McKinsey analysis

Rising costs threaten the system's sustainability. Washington's estimated total unfunded liability for Medicare (the federal government's health care program for the elderly) is a staggering $36 trillion.[1] A McKinsey analysis of Medicaid (the government program for the poor) finds that it will soon consume up to three-quarters of any new tax revenues in several US states, in effect crowding out spending on nearly all other social programs.

Nonetheless, the US system is also enviable in several ways. It is the world leader in health care research and innovation: more than two-thirds of all Nobel laureates in medicine over the past decade worked in the United States, and more than 80 percent of venture capital in the global health care sector flowed there in 2007. Publicly traded health care operations remain highly open to new business models and technological innovations.

What's more, health care services and technology are more readily accessible to insured patients in the United States than anywhere else. Wait times for elective surgeries, such as hip replacements, are up to three-quarters shorter than they are in nearly all other countries. About 40 percent of the world's medical travelers—people who go abroad to obtain acute elective care—come to the United States. And observers throughout the world recognize the distinctiveness of the system's treatment of diseases, such as cancer, that respond to technology and inpatient care.

Any proposal for fundamental health reform should seek to preserve and sustain these strengths while tackling the underlying factors that drive up costs—starting with the growing incidence of chronic lifestyle-induced diseases.

Reverse the growing incidence of chronic disease
In recent decades, the nature of medical risk in the United States has shifted dramatically. About two-thirds of all deaths in the United States now result from chronic diseases most often induced by behavior and lifestyle—for instance, obesity and related chronic conditions, type 2 diabetes and related conditions, smoking-related cancers, and alcohol-related liver disease. By contrast, before the 1940s or thereabouts, medical risk had largely been concentrated in random, infrequent, and catastrophic events such as injuries, congenital conditions, or contagious diseases. Health insurance was designed, at its inception, to address these kinds of events.

The increasing prevalence of chronic disease has significant implications for managing health care costs. For one thing, advances in

[1] According to the *2008 Annual Report of the Boards of Trustees of the Federal Hospital Insurance and Federal Supplementary Medical Insurance Trust Funds*, US Centers for Medicare & Medicaid Services (CMS).

medical technology and treatments mean that people with such conditions can now live much longer, though at a substantially higher financial cost. In fact, our findings suggest that the management of chronic disease outside of acute-care environments accounts for at least 20 percent of total US health care spending, perhaps more. That level of expenditure, compounded over decades in many cases, dwarfs the cost of end-of-life care—including, for example, the health care associated with the terminal stages of cancer or the last year of nursing-home care (Exhibit 2).[2] This point undercuts the cynical notion that chronically sick people die relatively young and therefore cost society less than people who receive health care services over the course of an extended lifetime.

For insurers—and ultimately employers—the changing nature of medical risk has big implications for risk pools. Pooling similar risks to provide protection against them underlies the concept of insurance, but commercial risk pools are becoming more and more asymmetric because they now bring together individuals presenting radically different risks. Meanwhile, employers are transferring more

[2] These findings reinforce the central role of preventing and managing chronic diseases but don't obviate the need to manage the costs associated with end-of-life care more effectively.

EXHIBIT 2

Living expenses

Lifetime health care spending in United States by age at death, $ thousand

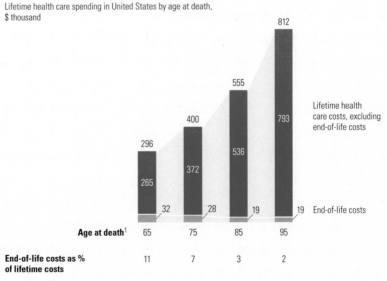

Age at death[1]	65	75	85	95
End-of-life costs as % of lifetime costs	11	7	3	2

[1] Figures for age 65 do not sum to total, because of rounding.

Source: Christopher Hogan, June Lunney, Jon Gabel, and Joanne Lynn "Medicare beneficiaries' costs of care in the last year of life," *Health Affairs*, 2001, Volume 20, Number 4, pp. 188–95; Gerald E. Riley and James D. Lubitz, "Trends in Medicare payments in the last year of life," *New England Journal of Medicine*, 1993, Volume 328, Number 15, pp. 1092–96; Bradley C. Strunk and Paul B. Ginsburg, "Tracking health care costs: Trends stabilize but remain high in 2002," *Health Affairs*, Web exclusive, June 11, 2003; US Centers for Medicare and Medicaid Services (CMS); McKinsey analysis

and more benefit costs to employees through premium sharing and other cost-sharing approaches. Healthier patients must therefore subsidize growing numbers of the chronically ill. This cross-subsidy in turn creates incentives for people in better health to forgo insurance, and that raises costs still higher for people remaining in the commercial risk pool. Together, these factors conspire to make health care less affordable and to increase the number of uninsured people in the United States.

When clinicians lead

James Mountford and Caroline Webb

The health care industry faces daunting challenges. Across developed countries, cost inflation continues unchecked, and profound quality and safety problems persist. Many health systems face recruitment challenges despite large pay raises for doctors, and an increasing number of clinicians say they would advise young people against choosing careers in medicine.

So further change is needed, despite years of progress in the quality of health care around the world. This transformation will require leadership—and that leadership must come substantially from doctors and other clinicians, whether or not they play formal management roles. Clinicians not only make the frontline decisions that determine the quality and efficiency of care but also have the technical knowledge to help make sound strategic choices about longer-term patterns of service delivery.

The conventional view of health care management divides treatment from administration—doctors and nurses look after patients, while administrators look after the organizations that treat them. Despite accumulating evidence of the positive impact of clinical involvement in the delivery and improvement of service, health care organizations often struggle to achieve this kind of participation. To understand the barriers to clinical leadership, we conducted interviews and workshops involving nearly 100 clinical professionals. Our research highlighted three main issues.

Ingrained skepticism

We found an ingrained skepticism among clinicians about the value of spending time on leadership, as opposed to the evident and immediate value of treating patients. Participants explained that playing an organizational-leadership role wasn't seen as vital either for patient care or their own professional success and therefore seemed irrelevant to the self-esteem and careers of clinicians. Moreover, many participants expressed discomfort with the idea that the impact of clinical leadership is often hard to prove.

One way to address this problem is to be far more systematic about gathering stories—told authentically and compellingly by those who participated in or observed them—that highlight the value of great clinical leadership. By "making heroes" of clinical leaders of all types, both in formal management and in frontline roles, organizations can create a stronger bank of role models and spark a sense of possibility.

Health care organizations need to build a solid, credible evidence base to show the importance of clinical leadership. While approaching the topic as though it were a clinical trial is difficult, organizations should track measures of clinical-leadership development and correlate them with their impact on quality and costs. To create

James Mountford is a consultant in McKinsey's London office, where **Caroline Webb** is a principal.

Obesity—a widespread chronic condition linked to others, such as diabetes, heart and circulatory maladies, orthopedic problems, and certain cancers—provides a telling example. The incidence of clinically defined obesity in the US adult population has more than doubled, to 34 percent, since 1980. The average annual cost of health care claims associated with morbidly obese patients (the fastest-growing category of obesity) is more than $7,500 a year, nearly twice the average for adults who are not obese (Exhibit 3). To put these figures in perspective,

this kind of evidence base, health care organizations need, at a minimum, basic performance data for making meaningful comparisons.

Weak or negative incentives

It became clear there were weak or even negative incentives for clinicians—especially doctors—to take on service leadership roles. Leadership potential generally isn't a criterion for entry into the clinical professions and often isn't a major factor in promotion. Nor is there a well-defined and respected career path for those with an appetite for formal leadership roles—in stark contrast with well-trodden clinical and academic tracks. Peer recognition is low or nonexistent, and often there are financial disincentives for doctors taking on organizational-leadership roles.

Policy makers and organizations must retune incentives. Correcting these problems is important not only for direct financial reasons but also because of the wider signals that incentives send about the value and prestige attached to clinical leadership. Where it flourishes, clinicians in formal leadership roles typically receive a small premium over colleagues who focus solely on direct patient care. Too great a financial premium, however, would make patient care less attractive and damage what ought to be the peer-to-peer relationship between leaders and other clinicians. As people come to appreciate the link between performance and enhanced clinical leadership, health systems can also encourage it indirectly by finding appropriate

ways to reward organizations that perform well and by creating meaningful consequences for those that don't.

Little provision for nurturing

We found little provision for nurturing clinical-leadership capabilities. Organizations generally lack meaningful processes for finding, inspiring, and stretching those clinicians who possess the greatest potential as leaders. Leadership and management training is frequently absent from core curricula for undergraduate or postgraduate trainees and for the continuing professional development of clinicians.

Any effort to encourage clinical leadership has to include support for professional development. Health care organizations must define what they want from their clinical leaders—what skills and attitudes they hope to encourage, whether there are differences across professions or roles, and where the need to develop leadership is greatest. They can then target their efforts wisely and help clinicians identify and overcome any shortcomings.

EXHIBIT 3

An expensive condition

Annual per capita costs for health care claims by body mass index (BMI),[1] United States, 2007, $

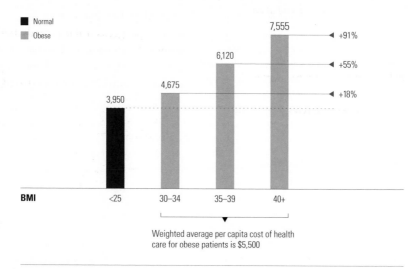

[1] For US adult population (ages 20–64); data for BMI of 25 to 29 (considered overweight, not obese) not shown.

Source: D2Hawkeye database of ~20,000 people with biometric data; National Bureau of Economic Research; US Census Bureau; McKinsey analysis

we estimate that the medical costs associated with clinically obese patients represent about 10 percent of the sum spent on health care premiums and that reducing obesity to the 1980 level would generate $60 billion a year in net savings.

Public and private institutions alike should collaborate to help reduce the overall incidence of obesity to 15 percent of the population over the next decade, as the US Centers for Disease Control and Prevention (CDC) suggests. The public side should mount a broad-based multi-institutional effort, comparable to those in recent decades to reduce tobacco consumption. The secretary of the US Department of Health and Human Services could convene and lead the effort, which should draw as needed on the broader resources of the government. Active participants should include public schools and the US Department of Education (nearly 20 percent of US children and adolescents are obese), the CDC, and the US Department of Agriculture.

A full-scale program to reverse the growing incidence of obesity should start with straightforward initiatives (for instance, to make it easier to bike along US roads) together with direct interventions (such as banning trans fats in foods). The country should also revive systematic efforts, like the Presidential Physical Fitness Award, to celebrate and encourage athletic activity among children. Comparable

"The childhood obesity epidemic won't be reversed unless we all are engaged—parents, schools, government at all levels, philanthropies, and the business community. The people and companies that grow food, develop food products, and market them must be a part of the solution."

— **Risa Lavizzo-Mourey,**
President and CEO,
Robert Wood Johnson
Foundation

The incidence of childhood obesity is soaring. To find out how the foundation is addressing the issue, read "Battling childhood obesity in the US: An interview with Robert Wood Johnson's CEO," on mckinseyquarterly.com.

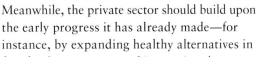

programs might then address other prevalent chronic conditions (for example, diabetes).

Meanwhile, the private sector should build upon the early progress it has already made—for instance, by expanding healthy alternatives in fast-food restaurants and improving the nutritional information on food packages. Companies could ultimately have a large, collective impact if they looked for new ways to help change the nutritional and exercise habits of Americans even in minor respects.

The stakeholders evaluating potential initiatives to counter chronic diseases should consider the influence of behavioral biases on decision making and build this understanding into the design of benefit plans and into prevention, wellness, and disease-management programs. In drug compliance efforts, for example, payers might harness the human tendency to overvalue positive short-term outcomes and to undervalue negative long-term ones. Behavioral economists at Carnegie Mellon University and the University of Pennsylvania recently designed an experiment along these lines.[3] Patients requiring drug therapy every day were significantly more likely to take their prescriptions when offered small daily financial rewards (namely, a chance to win a cash prize in a lottery). Meanwhile, noncompliant patients were advised how much they might have won had they complied. The experiment capitalized on the tendency to assign more significance to smaller punishments than to larger rewards.

In a different experiment, these same researchers found that when lower-calorie sandwiches appeared on the front page of a restaurant's menu, so that customers didn't have to hunt for them, an average order had 100 fewer calories than it did when such items were spread throughout the menu.[4]

Eliminate economic distortions
The US health care system is rife with economic distortions that impede value-conscious behavior by the suppliers and the consumers alike. This affects both the cost and quality of care. Any cost reduction initia-

[3]See Kevin G. Volpp, George Loewenstein, Andrea B. Troxel, Jalpa A. Doshi, M. Price, and Stephen E. Kimmel, "A test of financial incentives to improve warfarin adherence," *Biomedical Central: Health Services* Research, 2008, Volume 8, Supplement 1.
[4]See Kevin G. Volpp, Leslie K. John, Andrea B. Troxel, Laurie Norton, Jennifer Fassbender, and George Loewenstein, "Financial incentive-based approaches for weight loss: A randomized trial," *Journal of the American Medical Association*, 2008, Volume 300, Number 22, pp. 2631–7.

EXHIBIT 4

Luck of the draw?

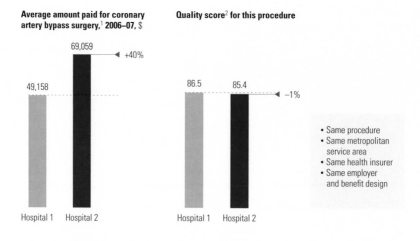

Average amount paid for coronary
artery bypass surgery,[1] 2006–07, $

Quality score[2] for this procedure

69,059 ◄ +40%

49,158

86.5   85.4 ◄ −1%

Hospital 1 Hospital 2   Hospital 1 Hospital 2

- Same procedure
- Same metropolitan
  service area
- Same health insurer
- Same employer
  and benefit design

[1] Based in internal mammary coronary artery bypass graft (CABG) surgery for patients admitted through the emergency room.
[2] US Centers for Medicare and Medicaid Services (CMS) composite quality scores.
Source: D2Hawkeye database of ~20,000 people with biometric data; CMS; McKinsey analysis

tive that ignores this fundamental disconnect will fail to make the system more sustainable in the long term. Without a more efficient, value-driven market, neither suppliers nor consumers have an incentive to prevent the kinds of decisions that are now undermining the system.

Today, for example, health care consumers—insurers, employers, patients, or others subscribing to insurance plans—find it extraordinarily difficult to discern or even define the benefits available at any given price and from any given provider and therefore cannot compare them. The lack of clear market signals also means that the service levels, practices, and even medical outcomes of the providers often bear little relation to their reimbursements (Exhibit 4). In no other industry are service attributes and prices so opaque.

To create a more value-conscious marketplace, it will be necessary to realign the funding of health services with the risks and behavior we wish to influence. On the demand side, consumers will have to become more responsible for their health care spending, for this would help mitigate the agency problem that currently hampers economically rational behavior and drives up costs throughout the system. Insured consumers simply don't understand the economic—and often quality— implications of the purchase decisions made on their behalf.

What might a value-conscious system look like in practice? One approach would be to have health insurance cover random, infrequent, and catastrophic risks beyond the control of individuals—for instance, nonelective hospital admissions, major surgery, and expensive therapies for cancer. Personal savings, out-of-pocket funds, or subsidies[5] could then contribute to payments for the more frequent, smaller, and predictable events, such as routine visits to physicians, certain postoperative visits, selected outpatient pharmaceuticals, and discretionary elective surgery. But strong incentives (for instance, waiving payment altogether) should encourage basic required health maintenance activities (for instance, getting a flu shot or other preventive measure). This approach would help to address a great imbalance: in 2007, nearly 60 percent of all US health care funding came from

[5] We recognize the need for effective subsidies to cover the costs of people who cannot pay for medical care, but the details of specific subsidy arrangements or schemes lie outside the scope of this article.

EXHIBIT 5

Imbalance in the system

US health care funding and costs by risk category, 2006, 100% = $1.878 billion,[2] %

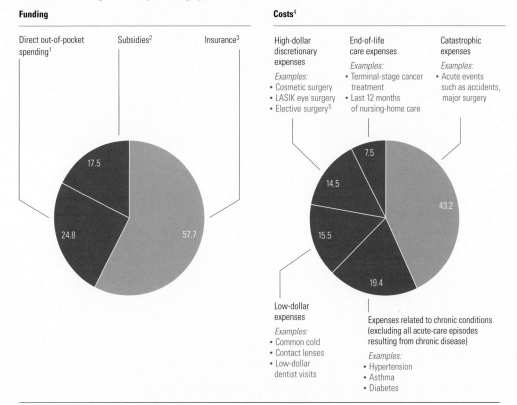

Funding

Direct out-of-pocket spending[1]

Subsidies[2]

Insurance[3]

17.5

24.8

57.7

Costs[4]

High-dollar discretionary expenses

Examples:
• Cosmetic surgery
• LASIK eye surgery
• Elective surgery[5]

End-of-life care expenses

Examples:
• Terminal-stage cancer treatment
• Last 12 months of nursing-home care

Catastrophic expenses

Examples:
• Acute events such as accidents, major surgery

7.5

14.5

43.2

15.5

19.4

Low-dollar expenses

Examples:
• Common cold
• Contact lenses
• Low-dollar dentist visits

Expenses related to chronic conditions (excluding all acute-care episodes resulting from chronic disease)

Examples:
• Hypertension
• Asthma
• Diabetes

[1] Includes federal and state subsidy programs, eg, Medicaid and State Children's Health Insurance Program.
[2] Includes copayment, coinsurance, and deductibles; excludes premiums for employer-sponsored and individually purchased insurance.
[3] Public and private employer-sponsored and individually purchased insurance, including consumer-paid premiums.
[4] Excludes government administrative expenses, structures, equipment, and public-health activities; does not include wellness expenses (eg, health club membership). Risk categories defined as: low dollar = $125 per instance (eg, prescriptions, dental care, vision care); high-dollar discretionary = ~$3,000 per instance; chronic = $118 per instance; catastrophic = $18,851 per instance; end of life = $32,763 per person per year of continuous care. Figures do not sum to 100%, because of rounding.
[5] Operations that, according to evidence-based medicine, do not yield better outcomes than other treatment methods (eg, back surgery, joint surgery).

Source: National health expenditure data, 2006, US Centers for Medicare and Medicaid Services (CMS); Medical Expenditure Panel Survey (MEPS), US Department of Health and Human Services; McKinsey analysis

How health care costs contribute to income disparity in the United States

Byron G. Auguste, Martha Laboissière, and Lenny T. Mendonca

Over the past 50 years, US workers have come to expect employers to pay for some part of employee health insurance; many consider this an important part of overall compensation. However, recent economic trends have resulted in a growing disparity in health care coverage and affordability. A study by the McKinsey Global Institute (MGI) identified three divergent categories of workers that are emerging from trends in health care coverage and income growth.

The top-income category (earning on average $210,100 annually[1]) has enjoyed rising incomes and growing employer-paid health care benefits, which have made their out-of-pocket spending on health care a relatively small and affordable portion of total spending. The higher-middle-income category (earning an average of $84,800 annually) and the lower-middle-income group (earning on average $41,500), have also seen increasing benefits and incomes—but at a much slower

Byron Auguste is a director in McKinsey's Washington, DC, office; **Lenny Mendonca** is the chairman of the McKinsey Global Institute, where **Martha Laboissière** is a consultant.

rate, making the uncovered portion of their health care costs ever more expensive. In the bottom-income category (earning an average of $14,800 a year), incomes have been stagnant, and their employers are less likely to pay for their health insurance. This group is finding any health care difficult, if not impossible, to afford.

As part of a study of widening income gaps between US households, we found that rising employer-paid health insurance premiums constitute a growing share of the combined income of lower-paid employees—a much larger share than for those who are higher paid. For those workers within the bottom-income group who are insured (22 percent), the ratio of employer-paid premiums to household income is 20 percent. That compares with 3.3 percent for the top-income group, in which nine out of ten workers are insured.

In addition, different income groups now experience strikingly different levels of health care coverage and benefits. Rising health care costs, reflected by spiraling insurance premiums, are widening the discrepancies between income groups in both the levels of

insurance, but only 43 percent of health care payments covered infrequent, random, or catastrophic events (Exhibit 5).

On the supply side, providers and regulators must move more quickly toward greater transparency. Evidence-based standards, such as the Core Measures established by the US Centers for Medicare and Medicaid Services (CMS), are a step in the right direction; to make information transparent to consumers, these standards track and report evidence-based data in areas such as the treatment of heart failure and the prevention of surgical infections. Medical societies or other third parties should intensify their efforts to propagate and enforce new metrics focusing on the appropriateness of care. That would aid the study of usage patterns and might therefore reveal over- or underdependence on certain technologies or services— say, expensive medical-imaging resources, such as CT (computerized tomography) scans, or clinical-laboratory diagnostics.

enrollment in employer-paid health schemes and insured workers' ability to afford premiums and out-of-pocket health care costs.

The latest available data, from 1996 to 2005,[2] shows that the average employer contributions to health insurance premiums grew 5 percent a year in real terms, to $5,068. Some employers are offering more comprehensive benefits to attract and retain better workers. At the same time, some companies have been prompted to withdraw the offer of employee health care benefits altogether; others have had to limit the number of employees eligible for benefits (for example, by including only full-time workers or those of a certain tenure). Employee contributions to insurance premiums have also been rising, discouraging some from taking up their employers' insurance offers altogether.

The authors wish to acknowledge Sara Parker for her extensive contribution to the research and article. They would also like to acknowledge Alexander Grunewald, James Kalamas, and Robin Matthias for their insightful input.

Such responses to rising premiums have resulted in stagnating or falling rates of enrollment in employer-paid schemes—a trend that has particularly affected middle-income employees. Put another way, employers are spending more on health care per employee but for fewer employees. In 2005, employer-paid health benefits covered 22 percent of households in the bottom-income group, contrasted with 56 percent of the lower-middle, 81 percent of the upper-middle, and 89 percent of the top-income group.

What's more, because incomes across the four groups of workers have been growing at such different rates in recent years, the average employer-paid premium for a worker in the top 10 percent was more than double the average for someone in the lowest 30 percent of income earners. Gaps in the extent of employer-paid health care services offered to employees at different income levels have thus widened. Employees benefiting from higher premiums receive a proportionately wider choice of health care goods and services.

[1] All average incomes are for 2005. The top-income group represents 10 percent of all households; the higher-middle-, lower-middle-, and bottom-income levels each make up 30 percent of the remainder.
[2] Analysis done for years comparable to available detailed household Current Population Survey (CPS) data.

The full version of this article is available on mckinseyquarterly.com.

Moreover, public and private stakeholders must agree upon—and report—standardized outcome metrics for both the effectiveness of clinical care (such as severity-adjusted mortality rates) and the incidence of egregious medical errors (including postsurgical infections and adverse drug reactions). These changes will make it easier to move toward a pricing system based on standardized care and, together with greater transparency, will help consumers compare providers and to judge the value and quality they offer. Transparency is particularly important for inpatient hospital care, which tends to be complex and hard to evaluate.

Ultimately, such moves would promote the widespread adoption of pay-for-performance reimbursement schemes and the further development of "infomediaries"—payers and other groups that help consumers make more informed decisions by providing information on prices, service, and quality. The government must play a central role by establishing reporting standards, specifying metrics, and creating similar reimbursement schemes for providers of care to government beneficiaries.

Simplify administrative complexity

Excessive administrative complexity is the third most important reason US health care is so costly. Research by the McKinsey Global Institute, for example, finds that in 2006, the bill for administrative costs in the United States came to nearly $500 per capita, nearly five times the average level across 13 other countries[6] in the Organisation for Economic Co-operation and Development (OECD). Further, we estimate that unnecessary administrative expenses currently represent fully 5 percent of total system costs, or about $100 billion a year.[7] This complexity comes primarily in two forms.

The first is the regulatory complexity imposed on payers in developing, distributing, and managing insurance products. Fifty different US state insurance commissions prescribe everything from basic mandates for minimum coverage to the format of enrollment forms to the language in marketing materials. Payers therefore have only a limited ability to distribute standardized products and thus benefit from economies of scale. Regulatory complexity also drives up costs in the payers' downstream operations by making it more complicated to process claims.

Related articles on mckinseyquarterly.com

Overhauling the US health care payment system

The retail revolution in health insurance

Innovation in health care: An interview with the CEO of the Cleveland Clinic

A second form of administrative complexity burdens transactions between payers and providers: the innumerable claims-management systems, IT platforms, reporting requirements, and contracting terms payers use. The average US hospital, for example, may work with 40 to 60 different payers, each with several products sporting unique contracting terms, reimbursement algorithms, and reporting requirements for quality metrics, productivity incentives, and so forth. Indeed, we find that US hospitals spend about 3 percent of their revenues just interacting with payers to deal with the problems created by this array of complexity.

As for payers, they incur unnecessary administrative costs as a result of the vastly different IT systems the thousands of providers they interact with use. Moreover, the providers don't characterize episodes of care in a uniform way and insist on contract terms with lots of

---

[6] Austria, Canada, Czech Republic, Denmark, Finland, France, Germany, Iceland, Korea, Poland, Portugal, Spain, and Switzerland.

[7] This figure is based on our analysis of administrative interactions between payers and providers, including both hospitals and physicians.

reimbursement levels and minor administrative distinctions. This too helps drive up complexity and costs.

To unravel this regulatory and administrative complexity, the public and private sectors must act aggressively to standardize key elements in the development, distribution, and management of insurance products and to make them more portable across states. While some progress has been made—for example, in creating consistent claims forms and codes—most administrative interactions still involve considerable variation. Public and private stakeholders alike should encourage the adoption of standards (akin to the bank-routing numbers that financial institutions use) to make these interactions faster and more efficient.

Both the public and private sectors might learn from the credit card industry, where third-party merchant processors handle both out-going requests for payment and settlement activities—roles divided in health care. Robust third-party utilities would let payers focus on creating innovative products to differentiate themselves, and providers on offering superior clinical outcomes at reasonable costs. Eventually, third-party utilities might handle a much larger range of activities, including insurance verification, performance management, contracting protocols, the coordination of benefits, and reconciliation.

Heightened collaboration between the public and private sectors will be crucial not only to curb administrative complexity but also to stem the rise of chronic diseases and ameliorate the pervasive economic distortions that ratchet up costs. Both sides bring important strengths to the table.

The authors wish to acknowledge the contributions of Steven Gipstein, Brian Hanessian, Kim Packard, Shubham Singhal, and Melanie Wyld.

We welcome your comments on this article. Please send them to quarterly_comments@ mckinsey.com.

Only the government can push all the levers available to increase the impact of the broad-based, multi-institutional programs that might cut the incidence of lifestyle-induced disease. Further, given the role of the government as both the largest purchaser of health services and the possessor of the largest fund of health-related claims data, it is also best placed to improve the transparency and exchange of information, as well as to trim the administrative complexity associated with poorly defined IT and data transfer standards.

The adaptability and nimbleness of the private sector allow it to help patients adopt healthier lifestyles—for example, through new approaches to managing chronic diseases. The private sector could also continue to create innovative financing products and to help patients receive superior care and service. ✚

Improving Japan's health care system

Japan needs the right prescription for
providing its citizens with high-quality health
care at an affordable price.

Nicolaus Henke, Sonosuke Kadonaga, and Ludwig Kanzler

On the surface, Japan's health care system seems robust. The country's
National Health Insurance (NHI) provides for universal access. Japan's
citizens are historically among the world's healthiest, living longer
than those of any other country. Infant mortality rates are low, and
Japan scores well on public-health metrics while consistently spending less on health care than most other developed countries do.

Yet appearances can deceive. Our research indicates that Japan's health
care system, like those in many other countries, has come under
severe stress and that its sustainability is in question.[1] The conspicuous
absence of a way to allocate medical resources—starting with
doctors—makes it harder and harder for patients to get the care they
need, when and where they need it. A vivid example: Japan's emergency rooms, which every year turn away tens of thousands who need
care. Furthermore, the quality of care varies markedly, and many
cost-control measures implemented have actually damaged the system's
cost effectiveness.

Nicolaus Henke is a
director in McKinsey's
London office; **Sono
Kadonaga** is a director
in the Tokyo office,
where **Ludwig Kanzler**
is an associate principal.

[1] For more detail on McKinsey's Japanese health care research, see two reports by the
McKinsey Global Institute and McKinsey's Japan office: "The challenge of funding Japan's
future health care needs," May 2008; and "The challenge of reforming Japan's health
system," November 2008, both available on mckinsey.com/mgi.

Meanwhile, demand for care keeps rising. For a long time, demand was naturally dampened by the good health of Japan's population—partly a result of factors outside the system's control, such as the country's traditionally healthy diet. Yet rates of obesity and diabetes are increasing as people eat more Western food, and the system is being further strained by a rapidly aging population: already 21 percent of Japan's citizens are 65 or older, and by 2050 almost 40 percent may be in that age group. Furthermore, advances in treatment are increasing the cost of care, and the system's funding mechanisms just cannot cope.

So Japan must act quickly to ensure that its health care system can be sustained. It must close the funding gap before it becomes irreconcilable, establish greater control over supply of services and demand for health care, and change incentives to ensure that they promote high-quality, cost-effective treatment. Many of the measures needed address a number of problems simultaneously and may prove instructive for other countries.

Japan's challenges

Underlying the challenges facing Japan are several unique features of its health care system, which provides universal coverage through a network of more than 4,000 public and private payers. All residents must have health insurance, which covers a wide array of services, including many that most other health systems don't (for example, some treatments, such as medicines for colds, that are not medically necessary).

The system imposes virtually no controls over access to treatment. There is no gatekeeper: patients are free to consult any provider—primary care or specialist—at any time, without proof of medical necessity and with full insurance coverage. Similarly, Japan places few controls over the supply of care. Physicians may practice wherever they choose, in any area of medicine, and are reimbursed on a fee-for-service basis. There is also no central control over the country's hospitals, which are mostly privately owned. These characteristics are important reasons for Japan's difficulty in funding its system, keeping supply and demand in check, and providing quality care.

Funding the system

Japan's health care system is becoming more expensive. In 2005 (the most recent year with available comprehensive data), the cost of the NHI plan was 33.1 trillion yen ($10.9 billion), or 6.6 percent of GDP.[2]

---

[2] Only medical care provided through Japan's health system is included in the 6.6 percent figure. However, if all of the country's spending on medical care is included, Japan's expenditures on health care took up 8 percent of its GDP in 2005.

By 2020, our research indicates, that could rise to 62.3 trillion yen, almost 10.0 percent of GDP, and by 2035 it could reach 93.6 trillion yen, 13.5 percent of GDP. True, the current cost—low by international standards—is projected to grow only to levels that the United States and some European countries have already reached. Yet funding the system is nonetheless a challenge, for Japan has by far the highest debt burden in the OECD,[3] a rapidly aging population, and a stagnating economy.

Why costs are rising. Four factors account for Japan's projected rise in health care spending (Exhibit 1). Advances in medical technology—new treatments, procedures, and products—account for 40 percent of the increase. The country's growing wealth, which encourages people to seek more care, will be responsible for an additional 26 percent, the aging of the population for 18 percent. The remaining 16 percent will result from the shifting treatment patterns required by changes in the prevalence of different diseases.

Japan can do little to influence these factors; for example, it cannot prevent the population's aging. Delays in the introduction of new technologies would be both medically unwise and politically unpopular. Yet unless the current financing mechanisms change, the system

[3] Organisation for Economic Co-Operation and Development.

EXHIBIT 1

Four underlying causes

4 factors[1] influencing projected increase in Japan's health care spending, trillion yen

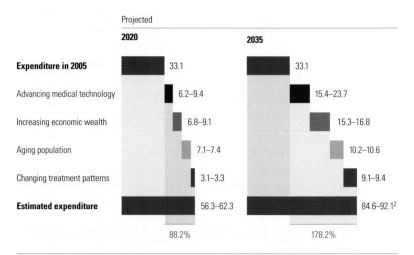

Projected

	2020	2035
Expenditure in 2005	33.1	33.1
Advancing medical technology	6.2–9.4	15.4–23.7
Increasing economic wealth	6.8–9.1	15.3–16.8
Aging population	7.1–7.4	10.2–10.6
Changing treatment patterns	3.1–3.3	9.1–9.4
Estimated expenditure	56.3–62.3	84.6–92.1[2]
	88.2%	178.2%

[1] The cross-effect of all four levers, estimated to be 3.4 trillion–5.4 trillion yen by 2020 and 12.9 trillion–16.3 trillion yen by 2035, is included in the estimates for each driver proportionately to the size of that driver.
[2] Figures do not sum to totals, because of rounding.

will generate no more than 43.1 trillion yen in revenue by 2020 and 49.4 trillion yen by 2035, leaving a funding gap of some 19.2 trillion yen in 2020 and of 44.2 trillion yen by 2035.

Compounding matters is Japan's lack of central control over the allocation of medical resources. No agency or institution establishes clear targets for providers, and no mechanisms force them to take a more coordinated approach to service delivery. Just as no central authority has jurisdiction over hospital openings, expansions, and closings, no central agency oversees the purchase of very expensive medical equipment. As a result, Japan has three to four times more CT, MRI, and PET scanners per capita than other developed countries do. Most of these machines are woefully underutilized.

No easy answers. Japan must find ways to increase the system's funding, cost efficiency, or both. Traditionally, the country has relied on insurance premiums, copayments, and government subsidies to finance health care, while it has controlled spending by repeatedly cutting fees paid to physicians and hospitals and prices paid for drugs and equipment. That has enabled Japan to hold growth in health care spending to less than 2 percent annually, far below that of its Western peers. At some point, however, increasing the burden of these funding mechanisms will place too much strain on Japan's economy.

If, for example, Japan increased government subsidies to cover the projected growth in health care spending by raising the consumption tax (which is currently under discussion), it would need to raise the tax to 13 percent by 2035. But the country went into a deep recession in 1997, when the consumption tax went up to the current 5 percent, from 3 percent. Similarly, a large spike in insurance premiums would increase Japan's labor costs and damage its competitive position. Markedly higher copayment rates would undermine the concept of health insurance, as rates today are already at 30 percent.

Even if Japan increased all three funding mechanisms to cover the system's costs, it risks damaging its economy. If copayment rates increased to 40 percent, premiums would still have to rise by 8 to 13 percentage points and the consumption tax by up to 6 percentage points (Exhibit 2). In the current economic climate, these choices are not attractive. Nevertheless, the country will have to resort to some combination of increases to cover the rise in health care spending.

Japan has repeatedly cut the fees it pays to physicians and hospitals and the prices it pays for drugs and equipment. This approach, however, is unsustainable. Fee cuts do little to lower the demand for health care, and prices can fall only so far before products become unavailable and the quality of care suffers. In addition, the country typically applies

EXHIBIT 2

No cheap fix

2035, trillion yen

Assumption No. 1: Copayment[1] remains at current level, 10–30%, depending on age and income level

Assumption No. 2: Copayment[1] increases to 40% across entire population

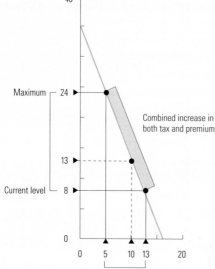

Average premium rate, %

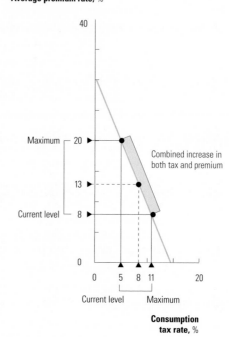

Average premium rate, %

[1] Copayment = direct mandatory contribution by patient to cost of treatment at point of care.

fee cuts across the board—a politically expedient approach that fails to account for the relative value of services delivered, so there is no way to reward best practices or to discourage inefficient or poor-quality care.

Mismatched supply and demand

Japan combines an excess supply of some health resources with massive overutilization—and shortages—of others.[4] On average, the Japanese see physicians almost 14 times a year, three times the number of visits in other developed countries. The introduction of copay-

[4] Japan does have a shortage of physicians relative to other developed countries—it has two doctors for every 1,000 people, whereas the OECD average is three. But when the number of physicians is corrected for disability-adjusted life years (a way of assessing the burden that various diseases place on a population), Japan is only 16 percent below the OECD average. Given the propensity of most Japanese physicians to move into primary care eventually, the shortage is felt most acutely in the specialties, particularly those (such as anesthesiology, obstetrics, and emergency medicine) with low reimbursement rates or poor working conditions.

ments and subsequent rate increases have done little to reduce the number of consultations; what's more, the average length of a hospital stay is two to three times as long in Japan as in other developed countries. In neither case can demographics, the severity of illnesses, or other medical factors explain the difference.

The country's health system inadvertently promotes overutilization in several ways. For starters, there is evidence that physicians and hospitals compensate for reduced reimbursement rates by providing more services, which they can do because the fee-for-service system doesn't limit the supply of care comprehensively. Japan's physicians, for example, conduct almost three times as many consultations a year as their colleagues in other developed countries do (Exhibit 3).

Furthermore, Japan's physicians can bill separately for each service— for example, examining a patient, writing a prescription, and filling it.[5] No surprise, therefore, that Japanese patients take markedly more prescription drugs than their peers in other developed countries. The system also rewards hospitals for serving larger numbers of patients and for prolonged lengths of stay, since no strict system controls these costs.[6]

Nevertheless, most Japanese hospitals run at a loss, a problem often blamed on the system's low reimbursement rates, which are indeed a factor. Another is the health system's fragmentation: the country has

[5] Many Japanese physicians have small pharmacies in their offices.
[6] Japan did recently change the way it reimburses some hospitals. Under the new formulas, they are paid a flat amount based on the patient's diagnosis and a variable amount based on the length of stay. The formulas do not cap the total amount paid, as most systems based on diagnosis-related groups (DRGs) do, nor do they cover outpatients—not even those who used to be hospitalized or will become hospitalized at the same institution. Thus, hospitals still benefit financially by keeping patients in beds.

EXHIBIT 3

Overutilization

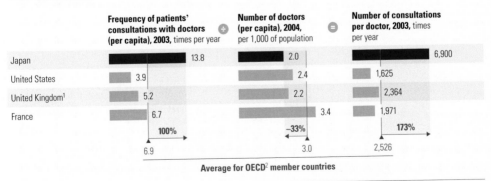

	Frequency of patients' consultations with doctors (per capita), 2003, times per year	÷	Number of doctors (per capita), 2004, per 1,000 of population	=	Number of consultations per doctor, 2003, times per year
Japan	13.8		2.0		6,900
United States	3.9		2.4		1,625
United Kingdom[1]	5.2		2.2		2,364
France	6.7		3.4		1,971
	100%		−33%		173%
	6.9		3.0		2,526

Average for OECD[2] member countries

[1] Data from National Health Service.
[2] Organisation for Economic Co-operation and Development.

Source: 2005 UK National Health Service; 2005 OECD health data (the most recent available for all member countries)

too many hospitals—mostly small, subscale ones. On a per capita basis, Japan has two times more hospitals and inpatients and three times more hospital beds than most other developed countries. Our analyses suggest a direct relationship between the number of beds and the average length of stay: the more free beds a hospital has, the longer patients remain in them.

Although Japanese hospitals have too many beds, they have too few specialists. One reason is the absence in Japan of planning or control over the entry of doctors into postgraduate training programs and specialties or the allocation of doctors among regions. Another is the fact that the poor economics of hospitals makes the salaries of their specialists significantly lower than those of specialists at private clinics, so few physicians remain in hospital practice for the remainder of their working lives. High consultation rates and prolonged lengths of stay exacerbate the shortage of hospital specialists by forcing them to see high volumes of patients, many of whom do not really require specialist care. As a result, too few specialists are available for patients who really do require their services, especially in emergency rooms. Japan has an ER crisis not because of the large number of patients seeking or needing emergency care but because of the shortage of specialists available to work in emergency rooms.

Quality of care

Given the health system's lack of controls over physicians and hospitals, it isn't surprising that the quality of care varies markedly. Among patients with stomach cancer (the most common form of cancer in Japan), the five-year survival rate is 25 percent lower in Kure than in Tokyo, for example. Four factors help explain this variability.

First, Japan's hospital network is fragmented. Research has repeatedly shown that outcomes are better when the centers and physicians responsible for procedures undertake large numbers of them. Because Japan has so many hospitals, few can achieve the necessary scale. In a year, the average Japanese hospital performs only 107 percutaneous coronary interventions (PCI), the procedure that opens up blocked arteries, for example. This is half the volume that the American Heart Association and the American College of Cardiology recommend for good outcomes. (In other developed countries, the average number of PCIs per hospital ranges from 381 to 775.) The small scale of most Japanese hospitals also means that they lack intensive-care and other specialized units. Few Japanese hospitals have oncology units, for instance; instead, a variety of different departments in each hospital delivers care for cancer.[7]

[7] One of the reasons most Japanese hospitals lack units for oncology is that it was accredited as a specialty there only recently. The country has only a few hundred board-certified oncologists.

Second, Japan's accreditation standards are weak. Doctors receive their medical licenses for life, with no requirement for renewal or recertification. No central agency oversees the quality of these physicians' training or the criteria for board certification in specialties, and in most cases the criteria are much less stringent than they are in other developed countries.

Third, the system lacks incentives to improve the quality of care. Japan has few arrangements for evaluating the performance of hospitals; for example, it doesn't systematically collect treatment or outcome data and therefore has no means of implementing mechanisms promoting best-practice care, such as pay-for-performance programs. Similarly, it has no way to enable hospitals or physicians to compare outcomes or for patients to compare providers when deciding where to seek treatment.

Finally, the quality of care suffers from delays in the introduction of new treatments. Specialists are too overworked to participate easily in clinical trials or otherwise investigate new therapies. And because the country has so few controls over hospitals, it has no mechanism requiring them to adopt improvements in care. Furthermore, the agency responsible for approving new drugs and devices is understaffed, which often delays the introduction or wide adoption of new treatments for several years after they are approved and adopted in the United States and Western Europe.

The way forward

There are no easy answers for restoring the vitality of an ailing health care system. Political realities frequently stymie reform, while the life-and-death nature of medical care makes it difficult to justify hard-headed economic decision making. If Japan, with all its unique features, can make progress in tackling its problems—funding, supply, demand, and quality—then other nations seeking to overhaul their health systems should pay careful attention both to the substance of its reforms and to the way it navigates the treacherous waters ahead.

The substance of reform

To close the system's funding gap, Japan must consider novel approaches. One possibility: allowing payers to demand outcome data from providers and to adopt reimbursement formulas encouraging cost effectiveness and better care. Another option is a voluntary-payment scheme, so that individuals could influence the amount they spend on health care by making discretionary out-of-pocket payments or up-front payments through insurance policies. Such schemes, adopted in Germany and Switzerland, capitalize on the fact some people are willing to pay significantly more for medical services, usually for extras beyond basic coverage. Our research shows that augmenting Japan's current system with voluntary payments could reduce the funding gap by as much as 25 percent as of 2035.

Japan could increase its power over the supply of health services in several ways. Incentives and controls can reduce the number of hospitals and hospital beds. One example: offering financial incentives or penalties to encourage hospitals (especially subscale institutions) to merge or to abandon acute care and instead become long-term, rehabilitative, or palliative-care providers. Similarly, monetary incentives and volume targets could encourage greater specialization to reduce the number of high-risk procedures undertaken at low-volume centers. The country should also consider moving away from reimbursing primary care through uncontrolled fee-for-service payments. Capitation, for example, gives physicians a flat amount for each patient in their practice.

Finally, the adoption of a standardized national system for training and accrediting specialists would be a critically important way to address Japan's shortage of them. Exerting greater control over the entry of physicians into each specialty and their allocation among regions, both for training and full-time practice, would of course raise the level of state intervention above its historical norm.

The demand side of Japan's health system invites greater intervention as well. Important first steps would include more strictly limiting services covered in order to eliminate medically unnecessary ones, as well as mandating flat fees based on patients' diagnoses to reduce the length of hospital stays. To encourage the participation of payers, the system could allow them to compete with each other, which would provide an incentive to develop deep expertise in particular procedures and allow payers to benefit financially from reform. They could receive authority to adjust reimbursement formulas and to refuse payment for services that are medically unnecessary or don't meet a cost effectiveness threshold.

Related articles on mckinseyquarterly.com

Universal principles for health care reform

Building Japan's generic-drug market

Addressing Japan's health care cost challenge

Another piece of the puzzle is to make practicing in hospitals more attractive for physicians; higher payment and compensation levels, especially for ER services, must figure in any solution. In addition, Japan's health system probably needs two independent regulatory bodies: one to oversee hospitals and require them to report regularly on treatments delivered and outcomes achieved, the other to oversee training programs for physicians and raise accreditation standards.

A process for reform

Awareness of the health system's problems runs high in Japan, but there's little consensus about what to do or how to get started. A productive first step would be to ask leading physicians to undertake a comprehensive, well-funded national review of the system in order to set clear targets. Such an approach enabled the United Kingdom's National Health Service to make the transition from talking about the problem of long wait times to developing concrete actions to reduce them.

Next, reformers should identify and implement quick wins—short-term operational improvements that produce immediate, demonstrable benefits—to build support for the overall reform effort, especially longer-term or politically contentious changes. A few success stories have already surfaced: several regions have markedly reduced ER utilization, for example, through relatively simple measures, such as a telephone consultation service combined with a public education campaign. Reform can take place in stages; it doesn't have to be an all-or-nothing affair.

The authors wish to acknowledge the substantial contributions that Diana Farrell, Martha Laboissière, Paul Mango, Takashi Takenoshita, and Yukako Yokoyama made to the research underlying this article.

We welcome your comments on this article. Please send them to quarterly_comments@ mckinsey.com.

Nor must it take place all at once. Indeed, shifting expectations away from quick fixes, such as across-the-board fees for physicians or lower prices for pharmaceuticals, will be an important part of the reform process. Significant departures from current practice would be needed to implement alternatives such as pay-for-performance programs rewarding physicians for high-quality care and penalizing them for inadequate or inefficient care, or the use of generic drugs through forced substitution or generic reference pricing, which would free up funds for new, innovative, and often more expensive treatments.[8] These measures will call for a significant communications effort to explain the reforms and show why they are needed.

Japan confronts a familiar and unpleasant malady: the inability to provide citizens with affordable, high-quality health care. By making the right choices, it can control health system costs without compromising access or quality—and serve as a role model for other countries. ✚

[8] Forced substitution requires pharmacies to fill prescriptions with generic equivalents whenever possible. Generic reference pricing requires patients who wish to receive an originator drug to pay the full cost difference between that drug and its generic equivalent, as well as the copayment for the generic drug.

Six ways to make **Web 2.0 work**

Web 2.0 tools present a vast array of opportunities—for companies that know how to use them.

**Michael Chui, Andy Miller,
and Roger P. Roberts**

Technologies known collectively as Web 2.0 have spread widely among consumers over the past five years. Social-networking Web sites such as Facebook and MySpace now attract more than 100 million visitors a month. As the popularity of Web 2.0 has grown, companies have noted the intense consumer engagement and creativity surrounding these technologies. Many organizations, keen to harness Web 2.0 internally, are experimenting with the tools or deploying them on a trial basis.

Over the past two years, McKinsey has studied more than 50 early adopters to garner insights into successful efforts to use Web 2.0 as a way of unlocking participation. We have surveyed, independently, a range of executives on Web 2.0 adoption. Our work suggests the challenges that lie ahead. To date, as many survey respondents are dissatisfied with their use of Web 2.0 technologies as are satisfied. Many of the dissenters cite impediments such as organizational structure, the inability of managers to understand the new levers of change, and a lack of understanding about how value is created using Web 2.0 tools. We have found that, unless a number of success factors are present, Web 2.0 efforts often fail to launch or to reach expected heights of usage. Executives who are suspicious or uncomfortable with perceived changes or risks often call off these efforts. Others fail because managers simply don't know how to encourage the type of participation that will produce meaningful results.

Some historical perspective is useful. Web 2.0, the latest wave in corporate technology adoptions, could have a more far-reaching organizational impact than technologies adopted in the 1990s—such as enterprise resource planning (ERP), customer relationship management (CRM), and supply chain management (Exhibit 1). The latest Web tools have a strong bottom-up element and engage a broad base of workers. They also demand a mind-set different from that of earlier IT programs, which were instituted primarily by edicts from senior managers.

Web 2.0 covers a range of technologies. The most widely used are blogs, wikis, podcasts, information tagging, prediction markets, and social networks (Exhibit 2). New technologies constantly appear as the Internet continues to evolve. Of the companies we interviewed for our research, all were using at least one of these tools. What distinguishes them from previous technologies is the high degree of participation they require to be effective. Unlike ERP and CRM, where most users either simply process information in the form of reports or use the technology to execute trans-actions (such as issuing payments or entering customer orders), Web 2.0 technologies are interactive and require users to generate new information and content or to edit the work of other participants.

EXHIBIT 1

The new tools

Adoption of corporate technologies

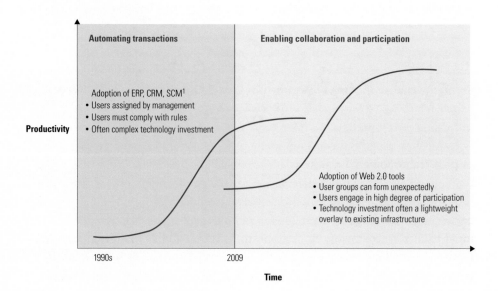

Automating transactions

Enabling collaboration and participation

Adoption of ERP, CRM, SCM[1]
• Users assigned by management
• Users must comply with rules
• Often complex technology investment

Productivity

Adoption of Web 2.0 tools
• User groups can form unexpectedly
• Users engage in high degree of participation
• Technology investment often a lightweight overlay to existing infrastructure

1990s

2009

Time

[1] ERP = enterprise resource planning, CRM = customer relationship management, SCM = supply chain management.

EXHIBIT 2

A range of technologies

Web 2.0 technology	Description	Category of technology
Wikis, commenting, shared workspaces	Facilitates cocreation of content/applications across large, distributed set of participants.	Broad collaboration
Blogs, podcasts, videocasts, peer to peer	Offers individuals a way to communicate/share information with broad set of other individuals.	Broad communication
Prediction markets, information markets, polling	Harnesses the collective power of the community and generates a collectively derived answer.	Collective estimation
Tagging, social bookmarking/filtering, user tracking, ratings, RSS[1]	Adds additional information to primary content to prioritize information or make it more valuable.	Metadata creation
Social networking, network mapping	Leverages connections between people to offer new applications.	Social graphing

[1] Really simple syndication.

Earlier technologies often required expensive and lengthy technical implementations, as well as the realignment of formal business processes. With such memories still fresh, some executives naturally remain wary of Web 2.0. But the new tools are different. While they are inherently disruptive and often challenge an organization and its culture, they are not technically complex to implement. Rather, they are a relatively lightweight overlay to the existing infrastructure and do not necessarily require complex technology integration.

Gains from participation

Clay Shirky, an adjunct professor at New York University, calls the underused human potential at companies an immense "cognitive surplus" and one that could be tapped by participatory tools. Corporate leaders are, of course, eager to find new ways to add value. Over the past 15 years, using a combination of technology investments and process reengineering, they have substantially raised the productivity of transactional processes. Web 2.0 promises further gains, although the capabilities differ from those of past technologies (Exhibit 3).

Research by our colleagues shows how differences in collaboration are correlated with large differences in corporate performance.[1] Our most recent Web 2.0 survey demonstrates that despite early frustrations, a growing number of companies remain committed to capturing the collaborative benefits of Web 2.0.[2] Since we first polled global executives

[1] Scott C. Beardsley, Bradford C. Johnson, and James M. Manyika, "Competitive advantage from better interactions," mckinseyquarterly.com, May 2006.
[2] "Building the Web 2.0 Enterprise: McKinsey Global Survey Results," mckinseyquarterly.com, July 2008.

EXHIBIT 3

Management 2.0

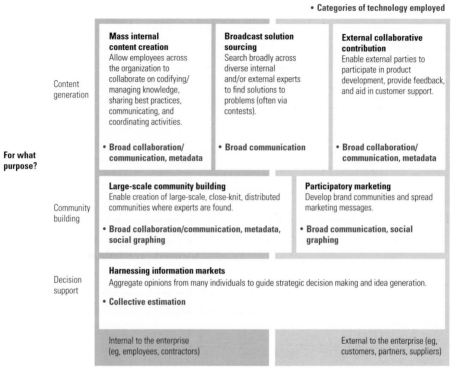

• Categories of technology employed

| | Content generation | **Mass internal content creation** Allow employees across the organization to collaborate on codifying/ managing knowledge, sharing best practices, communicating, and coordinating activities. | **Broadcast solution sourcing** Search broadly across diverse internal and/or external experts to find solutions to problems (often via contests). | **External collaborative contribution** Enable external parties to participate in product development, provide feedback, and aid in customer support. |

For what purpose?

Content generation
- Mass internal content creation — • Broad collaboration/ communication, metadata
- Broadcast solution sourcing — • Broad communication
- External collaborative contribution — • Broad collaboration/ communication, metadata

Community building
- **Large-scale community building** Enable creation of large-scale, close-knit, distributed communities where experts are found.
  • Broad collaboration/communication, metadata, social graphing
- **Participatory marketing** Develop brand communities and spread marketing messages.
  • Broad communication, social graphing

Decision support
- **Harnessing information markets** Aggregate opinions from many individuals to guide strategic decision making and idea generation.
  • Collective estimation

Internal to the enterprise (eg, employees, contractors) — External to the enterprise (eg, customers, partners, suppliers)

Who is participating?

two years ago, the adoption of these tools has continued. Spending on them is now a relatively modest $1 billion, but the level of investment is expected to grow by more than 15 percent annually over the next five years, despite the current recession.[3]

Management imperatives for unlocking participation
To help companies navigate the Web 2.0 landscape, we have identified six critical factors that determine the outcome of efforts to implement these technologies.

1. *The transformation to a bottom-up culture needs help from the top.* Web 2.0 projects often are seen as grassroots experiments, and leaders sometimes believe the technologies will be adopted without management intervention—a "build it and they will come" philosophy. These business leaders are correct in thinking that participatory technologies are founded upon bottom-up involvement from frontline staffers and that this pattern is fundamentally different from the rollout of ERP systems, for example, where compliance with rules is mandatory. Successful participation,

[3] See G. Oliver Young et al., "Can enterprise Web 2.0 survive the recession?" forrester.com, January 6, 2009.

however, requires not only grassroots activity but also a different leadership approach: senior executives often become role models and lead through informal channels.

At Lockheed Martin, for instance, a direct report to the CIO championed the use of blogs and wikis when they were introduced. The executive evangelized the benefits of Web 2.0 technologies to other senior leaders and acted as a role model by establishing his own blog. He set goals for adoption across the organization, as well as for the volume of contributions. The result was widespread acceptance and collaboration across the company's divisions.

2. *The best uses come from users—but they require help to scale.* In earlier IT campaigns, identifying and prioritizing the applications that would generate the greatest business value was relatively easy. These applications focused primarily on improving the effectiveness and efficiency of known business processes within functional silos (for example, supply-chain management software to improve coordination across the network). By contrast, our research shows the applications that drive the most value through participatory technologies often aren't those that management expects.

*Leaders sometimes believe the technologies will be adopted **without** management intervention—a "build it and they will come" philosophy*

Efforts go awry when organizations try to dictate their preferred uses of the technologies—a strategy that fits applications designed specifically to improve the performance of known processes—rather than observing what works and then scaling it up. When management chooses the wrong uses, organizations often don't regroup by switching to applications that might be successful. One global technology player, for example, introduced a collection of participatory tools that management judged would help the company's new hires quickly get up to speed in their jobs. The intended use never caught on, but people in the company's recruiting staff began using the tools to share recruiting tips and pass along information about specific candidates and their qualifications. The company, however, has yet to scale up this successful, albeit unintended, use.

At AT&T, it was frontline staffers who found the best use for a participatory technology—in this case, using Web 2.0 for collaborative project management. Rather than dictating the use, management broadened participation by supporting an awareness campaign to seed further experimentation. Over a 12-month period, the use of the technology rose to 95 percent of employees, from 65 percent.

3. *What's in the workflow is what gets used.* Perhaps because of the novelty of Web 2.0 initiatives, they're often considered separate from mainstream work. Earlier generations of technologies, by contrast, often explicitly replaced the tools employees used to accomplish tasks. Thus, using Web 2.0 and participating in online work communities often becomes just another "to do" on an already crowded list of tasks.

Participatory technologies have the highest chance of success when incorporated into a user's daily workflow. The importance of this principle is sometimes masked by short-term success when technologies are unveiled with great fanfare; with the excitement of the launch, contributions seem to flourish. As normal daily workloads pile up, however, the energy and attention surrounding the rollout decline, as does participation. One professional-services firm introduced a wiki-based knowledge-management system, to which employees were expected to contribute, in addition to their daily tasks. Immediately following the launch, a group of enthusiasts used the wikis vigorously, but as time passed they gave the effort less personal time—outside their daily workflow—and participation levels fell.

Google is an instructive case to the contrary. It has modified the way work is typically done and has made Web tools relevant to how employees actually do their jobs. The company's engineers use blogs and wikis as core tools for reporting on the progress of their work. Managers stay abreast of their progress and provide direction by using tools that make it easy to mine data on workflows. Engineers are better able to coordinate work with one another and can request or provide backup help when needed. The easily accessible project data allows

---

After this article was posted on our Web site, we encouraged users of Twitter—a microblogging and social-networking platform—to continue the conversation. Here are some of their responses, or "tweets."

Most respondents agreed that Web 2.0 work can't be added to an already full load, but instead needs to be meshed with everyday workflows.

@Salv_Reina: @McKQuarterly: re Workflow, this is critical. If the tool sits outside day 2 day work, it won't take easily #web2.0work

Some users raised questions about points in our analysis that they thought were missing or not fully developed.

@tomguarriello: @McKQuarterly: Yes, but your recs don't address the fear of social media that paralyzes many organizations. Loss of control/risk stops them

Others suggested where they thought we got it wrong.

@drkleiman: it feels like too much focus on the tools and tech itself, not enough on thinking thru strategy & goals that can be accomplished #web2.0work

Read more of their tweets on mckinseyquarterly.com.

senior managers to allocate resources to the most important and time-sensitive projects.

Pixar moved in a similar direction when it upgraded a Web 2.0 tool that didn't quite mesh with the way animators did their jobs. The company started with basic text-based wikis to share information about films in production and to document meeting notes. That was unsatisfactory, since collaborative problem solving at the studio works best when animators, software engineers, managers, and directors analyze and discuss real clips and frames from a movie.[4] Once Pixar built video into the wikis, their quality improved as critiques became more relevant. The efficiency of the project groups increased as well.

4. *Appeal to the participants' egos and needs—not just their wallets.* Traditional management incentives aren't particularly useful for encouraging participation.[5] Earlier technology adoptions could be guided readily with techniques such as management by objectives, as well as standardized bonus pay or individual feedback. The failure of employees to use a mandated application would affect their performance metrics and reviews. These methods tend to fall short when applied to unlocking participation. In one failed attempt, a leading Web company set performance evaluation criteria that included the frequency of postings on the company's newly launched wiki. While individuals were posting enough entries to meet the benchmarks, the contributions were generally of low quality. Similarly, a professional-services firm tried to use steady management pressure to get individuals to post on wikis. Participation increased when managers doled out frequent feedback but never reached self-sustaining levels.

A more effective approach plays to the Web's ethos and the participants' desire for recognition: bolstering the reputation of participants in relevant communities, rewarding enthusiasm, or acknowledging the quality and usefulness of contributions. ArcelorMittal, for instance, found that when prizes for contributions were handed out at prominent company meetings, employees submitted many more ideas for business improvements than they did when the awards were given in less-public forums.

5. *The right solution comes from the right participants.* Targeting users who can create a critical mass for participation as well as add value is

[4]See Hayagreeva Rao, Robert Sutton, and Allen P. Webb, "Innovation lessons from Pixar: An interview with Oscar-winning director Brad Bird," mckinseyquarterly.com, April 2008.
[5]Exceptions exist for harnessing information markets and searching crowd expertise, where formal incentives are an essential part of the mechanism for participation.

another key to success. With an ERP rollout, the process is straightforward: a company simply identifies the number of installations (or "seats") it needs to buy for functions such as purchasing or finance and accounting. With participatory technologies, it's far from obvious which individuals will be the best participants. Without the right base, efforts are often ineffective. A pharmaceutical company tried to generate new product ideas by tapping suggestions from visitors to its corporate Web site. It soon discovered that most of them had neither the skills nor the knowledge to make meaningful contributions, so the quality of the ideas was very low.

To select users who will help drive a self-sustaining effort (often enthusiastic early technology adopters who have rich personal networks and will thus share knowledge and exchange ideas), a thoughtful approach is required. When P&G introduced wikis and blogs to foster collaboration among its workgroups, the company targeted technology-savvy and respected opinion leaders within the organization. Some of these people ranked high in the corporate hierarchy, while others were influential scientists or employees to whom other colleagues would turn for advice or other assistance.

Related articles on mckinseyquarterly.com
The next step in open innovation
Succeeding at open-source innovation:
An interview with Mozilla's Mitchell Baker
Eight business technology trends to watch

When Best Buy experimented with internal information markets, the goal was to ensure that participation helped to create value. In these markets, employees place bets on business outcomes, such as sales forecasts.[6] To improve the chances of success, Best Buy cast its net widely, going beyond in-house forecasting experts; it also sought out participants with a more diverse base of operational knowledge who could apply independent judgment to the prediction markets. The resulting forecasts were more accurate than those produced by the company's experts.

6. *Balance the top-down and self-management of risk.* A common reason for failed participation is discomfort with it, or even fear. In some cases, the lack of management control over the self-organizing nature and power of dissent is the issue. In others, it's the potential repercussions of content—through blogs, social networks, and other venues—that is detrimental to the company. Numerous executives we interviewed said that participatory initiatives had been stalled by legal and HR concerns. These risks differ markedly from those of previous technology adoptions, where the chief downside was high costs and poor execution.

[6]See Renée Dye, "The promise of prediction markets: A roundtable," mckinseyquarterly.com, April 2008; and the video "Betting on prediction markets," mckinseyquarterly.com, November 2007.

Companies often have difficulty maintaining the right balance of freedom and control. Some organizations, trying to accommodate new Web standards, have adopted total laissez-faire policies, eschewing even basic controls that screen out inappropriate postings. In some cases, these organizations have been burned.

Prudent managers should work with the legal, HR, and IT security functions to establish reasonable policies, such as prohibiting anonymous posting. Fears are often overblown, however, and the social norms enforced by users in the participating communities can be very effective at policing user exchanges and thus mitigating risks. The sites of some companies incorporate "flag as inappropriate" buttons, which temporarily remove suspect postings until they can be reviewed, though officials report that these functions are rarely used. Participatory technologies should include auditing functions, similar to those for e-mail, that track all contributions and their authors. Ultimately, however, companies must recognize that successful participation means engaging in authentic conversations with participants.

Next steps

Acceptance of Web 2.0 technologies in business is growing. Encouraging participation calls for new approaches that break with the methods used to deploy IT in the past. Company leaders first need to survey their current practices. Once they feel comfortable with some level of con-trolled disruption, they can begin testing the new participatory tools. The management imperatives we have outlined should improve the likelihood of success. Q

The authors would like to acknowledge the contributions of their colleagues James Manyika, Yooki Park, Bryan Pate, and Kausik Rajgopal.

•

Michael Chui is a consultant in McKinsey's San Francisco office; **Andy Miller** is an associate principal in the Silicon Valley office, where **Roger Roberts** is a principal. Copyright © 2009 McKinsey & Company. All rights reserved.

We welcome your comments on this article.
Please send them to quarterly_comments@mckinsey.com.

Center Stage

A look at current trends and topics in management

Five trends that will shape business technology in 2009

Stefan Spang

When downturns hit, there is a certain inevitability to their impact on IT. Declining profits will place tremendous pressure on IT budgets in most sectors and regions. CIOs will be called on to rationalize projects, downsize organizations, renegotiate contracts, and seek out other cost reduction opportunities.

Much has changed, however, since the last big downturn, in 2001: technology budgets are larger, businesses have automated more processes, employees make greater use of tech-based productivity tools, and e-commerce has moved to the core of day-to-day operations. At the same time, IT organizations have established better mechanisms to govern IT decision making and have consolidated local IT operations to cut costs.

Taken together, this combination of cost pressures and IT organizations that are leaner, larger, and more vital to company goals will have new implications for business technology in 2009. Here's what may be in store.

1

IT and corporate finance converge

The year 2009 will be a tipping point for the CFO's involvement with IT. Large businesses have hundreds of millions or even billions of dollars locked up in their IT organizations—including data center facilities, systems assets, and organizational capabilities built over time. In a world where capital is at a premium, CFOs will seek to use IT assets as a lever to generate cash. They may sign outsourcing deals that include a bigger financing aspect, such as having IT service providers make a large up-front payment in return for higher margins over the course of a contract. They may sell and lease back hard assets, such as data center facilities. They may place favorable vendor financing at the core of hardware and software purchasing decisions, as many companies in heavy industry do when they buy industrial equipment and as telcos have done for years. Successful CIOs will give the senior-management team practical ideas on how to optimize cash.

2

Tension around IT budgets increases

Since 2001, IT capabilities have become ever more strategically important for most sectors. Yet IT budgets in many organizations will come under tremendous pressure in 2009, reducing investment for new business capabilities. Internal competition for rationed IT resources will become especially fierce as senior executives see access to them as critical to the success of their business units and their careers. Successful CIOs will have to position themselves as honest brokers, pushing hard to evaluate IT investments in a fact-based way yet avoiding any perception of being allied with one business unit or another.

3 The "last" IT project?

While it's clear that technological competence is critical in most industries, the variation in returns on IT investments is daunting. In retailing, for example, a CFO knows with some precision what an additional location will cost and how much revenue it is likely to generate. In contrast, an IT project's total cost could be off by an entire order of magnitude and its value either minimal or game changing. Senior executives at some organizations that have used IT less successfully in the past will probably throw up their hands and shut off all discretionary IT projects for the duration of the downturn. Naturally, this situation will challenge CIOs. The most effective course will be to explain what it would take to improve the value equation for IT investments.

4 Regulators demand more from IT

Government scrutiny of business will intensify in many developed countries. Already, in the United States, the Office of the Comptroller of the Currency weighs in on the resiliency of banking systems, the Food and Drug Administration (FDA) requires that many pharmaceutical systems be "validated," and Sarbanes–Oxley drives decisions about accounting systems in every industry. In the future, policy makers and regulators will probably demand that IT systems capture more and better data in order to gain greater insight into and control over how banks manage risk, pharma companies manage drugs, and industrial companies affect the environment. Government officials also will monitor many legal and business rules more closely to ensure compliance with mandates. Successful CIOs should enhance their relationships with internal legal and corporate-affairs teams and be prepared to engage productively with regulators. They will need to seek solutions that meet government mandates at manageable cost and with minimal disruption.

5 The offshoring and outsourcing landscape shifts

A decade ago, how many CIOs at Fortune 100 corporations would have guessed that Indian companies might now be among their largest and most strategic technology vendors? Just as the 2001 downturn led to a surge in offshoring, the 2008 downturn will also have far-reaching effects. A shake-up in the vendor landscape will likely follow the huge capacity increases of recent years, the current downward pressure on aggregate demand, and massive uncertainty in currency markets. Adding to the pressures are the strategic, government-sponsored initiatives launched by China and other nations to grab market share. Major mergers are more likely than not. New entrants will grow rapidly and some players could experience significant reverses. Successful CIOs will manage their vendor relationships as a portfolio so they will be well positioned as new winners evolve. CIOs will also need to be vigilant about how to manage transitions created by the consolidation or weakness of some service providers.

Stefan Spang is a director in McKinsey's Düsseldorf office. Copyright © 2009 McKinsey & Company. All rights reserved.

Artwork by Lloyd Miller

Cutting **sales costs,**
not revenues

Courageous companies can use the downturn to make their sales operations not only less expensive but also more effective.

**Anupam Agarwal, Eric Harmon,
and Michael Viertler**

There's a reason companies fear experimenting with the sales force: it is the engine that drives revenue. No matter how patched up or spluttering that engine may be, the thought of overhauling it fills senior executives with dread. To keep sales flowing, companies will make piecemeal ongoing repairs as long as they can.

Yet extraordinary economic times force companies to take every opportunity to cut costs and arrest declining revenues and margins. Unfortunately, fear and the belief that it isn't possible to be both fast and precise often result in two common mistakes: trimming only back-office staff and functions or instituting across-the-board cost cuts that include frontline sales reps. While both mistakes are understandable, they're likely to yield disappointing results.

Reducing back-office sales staff and functions in the belief that this will hurt revenues less than reducing the number of frontline sales reps may have worked in the past, but greater complexity has made support functions essential to effectiveness. Also, not all sales efforts are equal, especially in a downturn. It's crucial to determine where cuts will hurt customer perceptions and adversely affect their buying behavior; otherwise, important investments will be eliminated while low-value ones survive.

To avoid these mistakes, companies should consider a fundamentally different approach. First, examine the customer portfolio. How much effort really

Don Kilpatrick

goes into each customer and transaction? Which services does each of them need? What are their real profit margins? Which customers and markets are growing and which are shrinking? Understanding customers allows companies to focus sales resources where they are needed and to cut waste, not value. In fact, the sales force can become better *and* less expensive if organizations reject some traditional practices, such as assuming that big customers need or want big sales coverage, and embrace opportunities to become more efficient by sharing knowledge and resources.

This approach presents a change-management challenge, but economic times make it essential. In our experience, it helps companies to address most sales-related costs quickly and carefully, to cut them sustainably by 10 to 30 percent, and to minimize the risk of jeopardizing future growth.

Common pitfalls

A major telecom company wanted both to reduce sales force costs and to maintain its revenue. It decided to cut back-office support and protect the frontline sales staff—after all, executives reasoned, salespeople make sales. Unfortunately, while costs did fall, frontline sales reps began undertaking support tasks, such as creating reports, tracking orders, and developing sales materials. These additional duties, which reduced the amount of time that reps could spend with customers, weakened revenues. When managers realized what was happening, they began to circumvent the back-office hiring freeze by employing junior frontline sales staff to do back-office work.

Since even junior sales reps are on average more expensive than support staff, the result was the worst of both worlds: a less efficient yet more expensive support organization. What's more, embedding support roles within each region's frontline sales force meant that economies of scale were lost and best practices weren't shared. A few years later, the telco rethought its cost position and support infrastructure, essentially abandoning its sales force strategy. This was a tough lesson—and one that many companies should learn, for the telco was far from alone in thinking that it makes sense to insulate the frontline sales force from cost cuts.

The other common mistake is to cut sales force costs across the board, on the theory that if frontline and back-office resources decline equally, the result will simply be to increase the work burden on the remaining employees. But that isn't the only result. Cost cutting without regard to the profiles, importance, or potential of customers risks losing not only low-margin ones (which may be dispensable from an economic standpoint) but also their high-value counterparts. Meanwhile, the sales force may be left without the resources needed to capitalize on opportunities once the economy recovers.

Focus resources where they make a difference

There's a simple, overriding principle for companies to follow when they reduce their sales costs: do no harm. Small changes can have large unintended consequences, so companies must walk a fine line between reducing expenses and maintaining resources sufficient to protect current revenue and future growth. The key to these cuts is to be systematic—identify the effective sales channels; and promote efficiency in the sales organization.

Match sales resources with customers

Most companies base their allocation of sales resources on the size of the customer: big accounts generally get more coverage than little ones, though a few small, high-potential accounts get extra coverage. But imagine a different approach—one that takes into account the real profitability of each customer and the opportunity (size *and* growth) it represents and that distinguishes between highly complex, competitive transactions and simple ones. The reason to take this approach is straightforward: in most industries, the move that has the single biggest impact on sales force costs is adopting a sales model that makes desirable customers profitable to serve.

To gain a deep understanding of the needs and economic value of customers, companies must analyze the size, service costs, and true profitability of deals, not just their gross margins.[1] Some customers buy big, for example, but the cost of serving them leaves little room for profit. Others make small orders but are inexpensive to service and thus highly profitable. In addition, the trajectory of all customers is unique: you would usually prefer a growing to a shrinking one, and in these economic times you can't assume that any company is financially secure. Knowing how to find stable, profitable customers through micromarket targeting can help determine the appropriate sales channel and coverage model.[2]

Consider the case of a business-to-business (B2B) wholesale company, which found that as a result of its high-cost, face-to-face model for prospecting and managing accounts, only 45 percent of them were profitable. What's more, even its most profitable accounts could have been more so if it had invested in contract compliance and in efforts to make frequent contact with the people actually placing orders.

The company's response to this discovery was twofold. First, it moved all prospecting and account-management activities for smaller customers to telephone sales, with strong Web-based transaction support. That cut

---

[1] For more on establishing service levels, see Thomas Baumgartner, Roland H. John, and Tomas Nauclér, "Transforming sales and service," mckinseyquarterly.com, November 2005.
[2] For more on matching resources to micromarket opportunities, see David Court, "The downturn's new rules for marketers," mckinseyquarterly.com, December 2008.

total sales costs by more than half and doubled the number of profitable customers in this segment, to 90 percent. Second, for larger customers, the company assigned a team of telephone sales reps to contact the purchasing staffers who control individual orders. This move ensured that the people who actually make the daily buying decisions receive intensive service and reduced the senior managers' need for expensive face-to-face contact with procurement managers (Exhibit 1).

This story has two lessons. First, many customers don't want or need expensive face-to-face interaction. In fact, a shift to telesales may actually increase satisfaction and renewal rates for certain customers, which may otherwise have difficulty coping with inconsistent levels of face-to-face contact from sales reps preoccupied by larger accounts. For this B2B, the switch meant that the company not only got in touch with smaller customers more frequently but also understood their buying histories, which were immediately available on the desktops of telesales reps.

Second, the same customer may need more than one service channel. Winning a large account often requires the efforts of a senior manager supported by product specialists. But telesales reps may be better at maintaining accounts and driving penetration—an approach that both lowers service costs and improves customer satisfaction. For this wholesaler, the switch to telesales made local purchasers the primary point of contact and lessened the burden on procurement managers who negotiate big deals.

EXHIBIT 1

Customizing customer service

Business-to-business wholesale company (disguised example), %

■ Large customers
■ Small customers

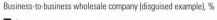

	Distribution of customers by size, %	Share of revenue, %
Large customers	25	85
Small customers	75	15

Impact

% of profitable customers per segment			Change, %	
From	70		Revenue growth	10
To		95	Savings in sales costs	5
From	45		Revenue growth	15
To		90	Savings in sales costs	40

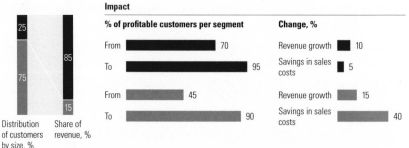

Initiatives	**Large customers**	**Small customers**
	• Moved transactional interactions (eg, order taking) to low-cost telesales, Web channels	• Moved small-account coverage to telesales with Web-based transactional support
	• Reduced senior managers' face-to-face contact with customers' procurement managers by moving this coverage to telesales	– Lower cost per transaction – Higher closing rates for previously underserved accounts

Stop wasting your sales reps' time

The primary task for any sales organization is to maximize the amount of time reps spend selling while ensuring that they sell the right products to the right customers. That's even more important during difficult economic times, when customers resist committing themselves and sales reps must pursue renewals and new business aggressively.

Freeing up the time of sales reps is easier said than done, however. The solution is to identify, understand, and eliminate anything that makes them less efficient. Most reps spend lots of time on non-revenue-generating activities, from customer service to administrative tasks such as travel and expense reporting. Many companies try to relieve that burden by hiring back-office staff—only to see back-office costs rise and sales productivity remain flat.

One retail power company took a different approach, creating a back office deliberately proportioned to undertake specific support activities and reviewing it every six months to ensure that it didn't become a sacred cow. The company also increased its sales quotas and coverage ratios—each sales rep's territory—to ensure that freed-up time was devoted to selling.

Making sure that sales reps sell isn't the only important thing. A less well-understood problem is focusing them on activities likely to drive results. Consider the experience of another B2B wholesaler that wanted to eliminate waste, variability, inflexibility, and other problems that diminish the revenues a sales force can generate. First, the company made its sales process and reps more efficient by creating a model to predict the needs and spending of customers. Using information such as their size, industries, and previous buying histories, the model ranked them by opportunity. It also provided reps with weekly reports to ensure that they focused on products clients were likely to buy.

Meanwhile, the company sought to make the performance of its sales reps less variable by improving the productivity of low performers through the sharing of best practices. Sales reps were now encouraged to follow a standard operating model, including weekly schedules for interacting with customers, pocket guides and tools, and sales call templates. For many salespeople, adopting such practices required a significant change in mind-set and behavior, so the transformation included efforts to identify role models and comprehensive training in communications to reinforce systems and processes (see sidebar, "Managing sales force change in tough times"). As a result of these changes, the company reduced the number of sales reps by 12 percent and is on track to increase revenue by as much as 30 percent.

Ensure that presales support delivers "best thinking" consistently

Most companies provide some level of bid and pricing support, but few treat it strategically. As a result, small groups of decentralized sales support staffers—or even sales reps themselves—prepare for initial discussions with prospective customers or fill out responses to bids and requests for proposals. This is hardly the most effective approach: because individual reps and teams see only a small fraction of a company's interactions, they may fail to use its best thinking.

A large IT service provider tackled this problem by creating a centralized group to drive costs down and effectiveness up. A small, highly skilled team within the group prepared key bids and monitored conversion rates. Another part of it conducted win–loss reviews to understand why bids did or didn't work, how competitors positioned themselves against the company, and how customers responded to that positioning. Using insights from the review process, yet another team in the centralized group prepared highly effective, simple-to-use internal training and marketing materials (Exhibit 2).

This approach has two compelling benefits. First, it increases win rates by using the whole company's best thinking, drawn from experience with similar offerings (and those of competitors) across the sales cycle. Second, it lowers costs by ensuring that key proposals and materials are prepared

E X H I B I T   2

A standard operating model

IT service example

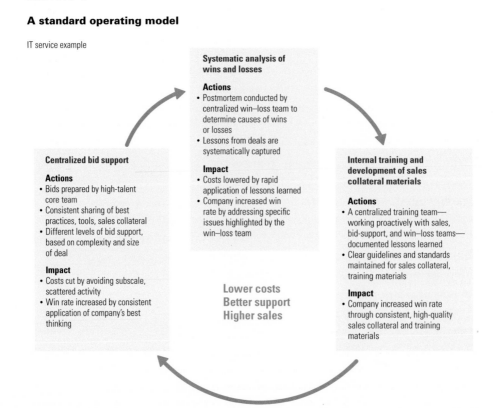

Systematic analysis of wins and losses

Actions
- Postmortem conducted by centralized win–loss team to determine causes of wins or losses
- Lessons from deals are systematically captured

Impact
- Costs lowered by rapid application of lessons learned
- Company increased win rate by addressing specific issues highlighted by the win–loss team

Centralized bid support

Actions
- Bids prepared by high-talent core team
- Consistent sharing of best practices, tools, sales collateral
- Different levels of bid support, based on complexity and size of deal

Impact
- Costs cut by avoiding subscale, scattered activity
- Win rate increased by consistent application of company's best thinking

Internal training and development of sales collateral materials

Actions
- A centralized training team—working proactively with sales, bid-support, and win–loss teams—documented lessons learned
- Clear guidelines and standards maintained for sales collateral, training materials

Impact
- Company increased win rate through consistent, high-quality sales collateral and training materials

Lower costs
Better support
Higher sales

centrally rather than forcing people in the field to reinvent them continually. Both benefits are now critical, for tight budgets make it even more important to focus sales resources on the best opportunities, and superior information can make all the difference.

Squeeze out inefficiencies after the sale

Companies shouldn't relax after winning business, when they undertake tasks such as provisioning and reporting orders. An inefficient postsales

---

Managing sales force change in tough times

Tough economic times make many workers uncomfortable; they crave stability, not upheaval. Salespeople are hardly different, and they present unique challenges that complicate change efforts even in the best of times. First, they're independent and entrepreneurial; they tend to act primarily in their own and their customers' best interests. Second, the decentralized nature of a sales organization makes it harder to communicate, coordinate, and adopt changes. Finally, companies must shepherd a number of stakeholders with divergent objectives—frontline reps, back-office support, customers, channel partners, and managers, for example—through any transformation. The companies that are most successful at overcoming these obstacles concentrate on a few tactics.

Articulate and communicate the value of change for everyone. A medical-product company, for example, wanted to underline the value created by shifting low-priority accounts to telesales and freeing up time for salespeople to pursue higher-priority accounts. It therefore changed the sales reps' compensation structure to emphasize those accounts.

Tailor the new sales strategy at the local level. Change imposed from above makes employees nervous. To avoid that outcome, a global high-tech manufacturer involved managers from more than 30 countries in adapting its strategy to local conditions and conducted workshops that clarified the strategy's relevance for sales reps in each region.

Create demand pull from the front line. The medical-product company generated enthusiasm through a pilot program assigning a telesales team to support sales reps. They soon had 30 percent more time to spend on high-potential accounts because of the burden picked up by the telesales team, which quickly achieved conversion rates equal to or higher than theirs. Within a few months, salespeople were clamoring to join the program. Although it was initially deployed across only 25 percent of the company, it accounted for a substantial increase in returns on sales and was rolled out to the rest of the organization within the year.

Measure and reward change. To alleviate the anxiety that can accompany change, companies must reassure employees that those who embrace change will be rewarded. Both the high-tech and medical-product companies carefully tracked the performance of the sales reps, tied their incentives to transition milestones, and aligned their compensation with clear targets. These companies also made sure that everyone knew—and celebrated—when the sales organization met critical goals.

Use the change process to upgrade capabilities. Not everyone can change. Another medical-product company found that about a third of its sales force had the ability and will to do so, another third was willing to try, and the remainder declined to participate. Over time, sales reps viewed the departure of their recalcitrant colleagues as a positive step that helped the company recruit new talent to make the organization stronger.

Laura Furmanski is an associate principal in McKinsey's Silicon Valley office, and **Rodolfo Luzardo** is an associate principal in the Miami office.

back office not only diminishes the quality of customer service but is also costly, both directly and because it forces frontline reps to spend time correcting mistakes. Consider the experience of a large European telecom provider that expended about 3 days of actual work time on its order process, though it lasted about 47 days from end to end. The company's analysis revealed that less than 60 percent of the activities in the process added value.

Eliminating the waste called for two major changes. First, the company segmented its back office to separate high-value, high-complexity issues from low-value, low-complexity ones. That separation, allowing basic sales to flow through a less rigorous process, lowered the number of exceptions and other special requests. More-complex deals were handled appropriately, reducing error rates and rework. Second, the company minimized handoffs by cross-training people and reducing the number of single-function departments. Wait times between handoffs fell and the quality of the work improved as a feeling of ownership over the process increased. The bottom line was that operational metrics improved significantly: work-in-progress orders fell by 60 percent, the order backlog by 84 percent, and lead times by 29 percent; overall productivity rose by 295 percent (Exhibit 3).

Getting started

Sales teams typically resist change; they not only worry that it will imperil relationships with clients and revenue but also wonder why a company

EXHIBIT 3

Efficiencies after the sale

Telco example

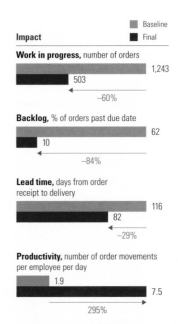

would risk tinkering with a sales force that gets the job done, even imperfectly. These teams fear the unknown rather than change itself. And the unknown is particularly frightening today: the order books of many sales reps are drying up, and their bonuses—and sometimes jobs—are on the line.

What if sales teams knew that change would improve customer satisfaction and retention or that profit margins would widen, sales costs fall, and compensation increase? Suppose they knew that frontline reps would get more time to sell, while back-office resources would be focused more appropriately? Most important, what if they realized that companies can make changes quickly yet thoughtfully? Speed is crucial during a downturn, but the pressure to act contributes to poor, rushed decisions.

Being thoughtful needn't mean being slow: many companies can identify cost-saving opportunities and settle on an implementation strategy in less than three months. In fact, a few things can happen immediately. They include testing to find telesales opportunities; having the sales force carry out a detailed time accounting for one to two weeks to learn where selling capacity is used; centralizing the preparation of bids (in particular, sharing successful bid information, a move that often quickly curbs unneeded price discounting); and investigating key postsales processes to determine the number of handoffs. Such moves have helped many companies find quick wins that make sales-improvement efforts self-funding within two quarters.

Related articles on mckinseyquarterly.com
The downturn's new rules for marketers
Rapid transformation of a sales force
Managing a marketing and sales transformation

This approach also helps focus near-term priorities. Not everything must be done at once, and some things may not have to be done at all. A company's specific actions depend on several factors, including its current state, as well as its need and capacity for change. Some companies may realize the bulk of their savings by matching sales resources with customers more appropriately. Others may already have finely tuned sales channels but benefit from centralizing support resources. In fact, there's perhaps only one universal truth: being smarter about the way a company cuts its sales force costs greatly improves the odds of success. Q

The authors wish to acknowledge the contributions of Maria Valdivieso de Uster to this article.

•

Anupam Agarwal is an associate principal in McKinsey's Silicon Valley office, **Eric Harmon** is a principal in the Dallas office, and **Michael Viertler** is a principal in the Munich office.

We welcome your comments on this article.
Please send them to quarterly_comments@mckinsey.com.

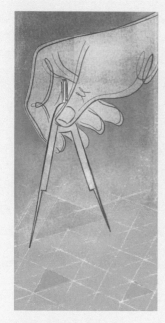

87
Mapping decline and recovery across sectors

92
Upgrading R&D in a downturn

95
High tech: Finding opportunity in the downturn

The crisis: Staying ahead of your competitors

Artwork by Don Kilpatrick

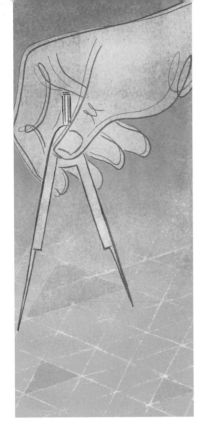

Mapping decline and recovery across sectors

Different sectors enter and emerge from downturns at different times. A look at past recessions suggests how some industries may fare.

Bin Jiang, Timothy M. Koller, and Zane D. Williams

In an ideal world, every company would enter a recession led by a team of grizzled executives who could draw on their experiences of past downturns to guide it through the current one. Many companies don't, however, and even for those that do, it can be difficult to rise above the crisis to ponder the lessons of history. Yet in a recession, developing accurate strategic plans is usually a high-stakes effort. False assumptions about the pace, scale, and timing of growth may slow progress in good times but could be fatal now.

Executives in an industry that lags behind the economy, for example, may imagine that they can avoid a downturn because at first the industry doesn't slow down when the economy does. Other executives, failing to realize that their industries tend to revive before the overall economy, may plan too conservatively for the upturn. Decisions about acquisitions, divestitures, and even recruiting or retaining talent often hang in the balance.

To help executives sharpen their perspective, we looked at the financial performance of US companies during the four most recent recessions.[1]

Tim Koller is a principal in McKinsey's New York office, where **Bin Jiang** and **Zane Williams** are consultants.

[1] The recessions we studied were those of November 1973–March 1975, January 1980–November 1982, July 1990–March 1991, and March 2001–November 2001. Technically, the 1980–82 downturn was two recessions: January 1980–July 1980 and July 1981–November 1982. For this analysis, we have combined the two.

Then we analyzed sector-level[2] total returns to shareholders (TRS), revenue growth, and growth in earnings before interest, taxes, and amortization (EBITA) around the times of these downturns. Although such analyses can't provide definitive parallels from one recession to the next (for obvious reasons, such as size, geographical reach, or origins), the general trends can prove invaluable in helping executives examine their assumptions about the future performance of an industry. We found that, so far at least, the current recession—despite claims of its being unprecedented—seems to be following many of the patterns that previous ones did.

[2] We grouped the companies in our sample into ten Global Industry Classification Standards (GICS) sectors.

EXHIBIT 1

True to type

Sequence of sector decline and recovery[1]

■ Lead ■ Lag ■ In line □ No effect

Sector	Downturn 1973–75[2]	1980–82	1990–91	2001	Q3 2008	Recovery 1973–75[2]	1980–82	1990–91	2001	Q3 2008
Consumer discretionary										?
Consumer staples					?					?
Energy					?					?
Financial[3]					?					?
Health care					?					?
Industrial										?
Information technology					?					?
Materials					?					?
Telecommunications services					?					?
Utilities				N/A[4]	?				N/A[4]	?

[1] Recovery is defined as 1st quarter of sustainable, positive real earnings before interest, taxes, and amortization (EBITA) growth following quarter in which it bottoms out; in line means occurring within 1 quarter before or after beginning or end of the recession; no effect is defined as <10% decline in real EBITA. Question marks indicate sectors where, as of Q3 2008, there was no significant change in EBITA.
[2] Based on annual data.
[3] Categorized by decline in real net interest income.
[4] Utilities not meaningful in 2001, because of impact of idiosyncratic events (eg, Enron collapse) unrelated to recession.

• *Similar beginnings.* The timing of contractions in sector-level sales and EBITA indicates that the four most recent recessions began with a core underlying shock that then spread through the economy in a fairly predictable way. All four began with falling sales and EBITA in the consumer discretionary sector, and three began with similar declines in the IT sector as well (Exhibit 1). By contrast, in three of the four, the energy sector was among the last to be hit. Some sectors have been fairly resistant to recessions: consumer staples wasn't affected significantly in the last three, and the last two didn't significantly affect health care.

• *Variable magnitude.* The size of the contraction in EBITA varies across sectors (Exhibit 2). Generally, consumer discretionary, materials, energy, and industrial post the sharpest drops. The information technology sector has been more variable, with large drops during the past two recessions but smaller ones in 1973–75 and 1980–82. The most resilient sectors have been health care and consumer staples, whose revenues and EBITA fell relatively little in the majority of the previous recessions.

• *The speed of decline and recovery.* In almost every recession we studied, sectors contracted much more quickly than they recovered.[3]

[3]Of the 27 instances when we documented a decline in earnings before interest, taxes, and amortization (EBITA) due to a recession, 24 showed a drop in EBITA that was faster than the recovery.

EXHIBIT 2

Varied effects

Degree of sector declines in EBITA[1] during recessions

Sector	Peak-to-trough change, %			
	1973–75[2]	1980–82	1990–91	2001
Consumer discretionary	−71	−62	−47	−36
Consumer staples	−38	−5	6	−5
Energy	−23	−38	−51	−55
Financial[3]	−8	22	−15	−9
Health care	−17	−31	2	21
Industrial	−13	−48	−46	−26
Information technology	−13	−11	−35	−99
Materials	−33	−72	−62	−44
Telecommunications services	−6	−57	−8	−45
Utilities	−5	−5	−8	−20

[1]Earnings before interest, taxes, and amortization.
[2]Based on annual data.
[3]Categorized by decline in real net interest income.

EXHIBIT 3

Less variability in share prices

Total returns to shareholders (TRS) decline by sector

Sector	1973–75[1]	1980–82	1990–91	2001
Consumer discretionary	−54	−15	−30	−42
Consumer staples	−38	−10	−10	−12
Energy	−35	−38	−7	−24
Financial	−56	−13	−35	−18
Health care	−39	−9	−5	−52
Industrial	−47	−6	−20	−26
Information technology	−49	−10	−15	−76
Materials	−26	−7	−15	−15
Telecommunications services	−40	−6	−20	−76
Utilities	−41	−8	−10	−39

[1] Based on annual data.

Typically, it takes six to eight quarters for a sector's EBITA to bottom out—fewer in 1973–75 and more in 1980–82. The time needed to get back to peak EBITA levels generally is not only much longer but also highly variable. It took the better part of a decade for many sectors to recover from the recession of the early 1980s. After the recession of 2001, however, it took just over two years for most sectors to recover their peak EBITA levels once they reached bottom. Some industries, such as telecommunications in 2001, never hit their peak levels again.

• *Similarities in share price performance.* Share prices tend to decline either before or just as a recession starts; rarely does a sector's TRS begin to decline much later. As a result, the share price performance of different sectors during a recession tends to be more similar than their financial performance (Exhibit 3). Share prices also tend to rise in step near the end of a recession, in marked contrast to revenues and EBITA, which often lag behind significantly.

Overall, the impact of recessions on share prices has varied. During the 1973–75 downturn (and to a lesser extent, the 2001 one), share prices fell steeply, with many sectors suffering large losses; in 1973–75, for instance, all sectors but materials (which was down by 26 percent) lost more than a third of their value. In the 2001 recession, seven out of ten sectors lost more than 20 percent of their value. Sectors affected by "shocks" can fare even worse: IT and telecommunications each lost more than 75 percent of their value in the recession of 2001.

The 1980–82 and 1990–91 recessions affected valuations less severely. Only one sector lost more than a third of its value in either downturn (energy in 1980–82 and financial in 1990–91), and most sectors suffered losses of 5 to 15 percent.

The current recession seems to be following many patterns we observed in its predecessors. The consumer discretionary sector, which is sensitive to economic decline, has led in all of the past four recessions. It is also leading the current downturn, having posted the sector's largest post-2001 drop in EBITA—almost 5 percent—during the second quarter of 2007, five months before the recession's official start.[4]

In 2008, TRS fell significantly in nearly every sector, with all but consumer staples losing more than 20 percent of their value and seven losing more than a third of it.[5] Given the historical patterns (and current headlines), revenues and EBITA can be expected to fall in most other sectors as the recession continues. These similarities give executives some idea of what to expect as they plan their next steps.

History also suggests some possible indicators of the beginning of a recovery. In three of the four most recent recessions, higher consumer discretionary and IT spending led the way. When real EBITA growth resumes in these sectors, it may be a useful indication that the economy is turning around. Also, TRS generally stops declining near the end of a recession, so resumed growth in broad stock market indices might also herald the end of the current one. Q

---

[4] The National Bureau of Economic Research has dated the start of the current US recession as December 2007.
[5] The 2008 total returns to shareholders (TRS) measured as of November 30, 2008.

Upgrading R&D in a downturn

Cutting research costs across the board in a recession isn't smart. Companies should use R&D as an opportunity to make themselves more competitive.

Christie W. Barrett, Christopher S. Musso, and Asutosh Padhi

As the global economic downturn spurs companies to slash costs, many senior executives are intensely scrutinizing research-and-development budgets. In fact, R&D is a perennially attractive target for corporate belt-tightening rituals, since it doesn't produce cash directly. Now more than ever, many companies are trying to generate quick savings—and to spread the pain of cutbacks in an equitable way—by asking their development groups to cut costs across the board.

Yet such tempting reductions starve and therefore delay promising projects while allowing unworthy "zombie" ones to linger. Worse, wholesale layoffs destroy morale among the remaining staff and can even prod your very best development engineers, who are always in demand, to accept the severance package that may be on offer and move elsewhere. Companies should take a more strategic approach to cutting R&D costs, by using today's difficult economic environment as an opportunity to upgrade the R&D organization's focus, practices, and management. That path helps companies not only to cut their costs but also to raise productivity and speed up time to market—while positioning themselves for even greater success in the future.

Christie Barrett is a consultant in McKinsey's Detroit office, **Chris Musso** is an associate principal in the Cleveland office, and **Asutosh Padhi** is a principal in the Chicago office.

For most organizations, the first step is to examine the R&D portfolio rigorously to accelerate the most strategically promising projects while canceling irrelevant or moribund ones. It would seem obvious that companies ought to be doing this all the time, but many resist because of the challenges. Portfolios often grow organically, for example, with little central oversight, so it can be difficult for senior executives at a large company to get their arms around the totality, let alone the expected value, of its R&D activities. Another challenge: targeting specific projects for elimination means having difficult conversations with the people who lead them. It's far easier to ask for sweeping cuts.

Many undermanaged and drifting underperformers survive these broad cuts, however. In large companies, such projects may even go unnoticed as changing market conditions undermine them. One leading industrial company, for instance, recently discovered, during a portfolio review, that the technology of a large project launched five years earlier had been eclipsed by the offerings of more nimble competitors.

Nasty surprises like this are common. Our experience in industries such as automotive, energy and basic materials, high tech, and medical devices suggests that all but the most vigilant product developers could terminate one-quarter to one-third of their projects, liberating resources for redeployment. For a typical consumer-focused manufacturer with $5 billion in revenues and $250 million in annual R&D expenditures, the value at stake represents nearly 2 percent of sales. Such a strategic review frees up not only resources but also management attention, which a company can use to tear down silos, boost crossfunctional collaboration, and manage R&D actively as a portfolio.

A chemical maker, for example, reduced the time to market of its top R&D project by more than 12 months and added more than $100 million to the net present value of its R&D portfolio. How? It killed three zombie projects, redeployed resources to accelerate the development of its most promising new product, and improved early-stage R&D collaboration between engineers and marketers so that executives could make better decisions about which efforts to finance.

Companies can also make their development efforts more effective by infusing them with lean-management principles. While lean thinking is commonplace in manufacturing environments, most companies, fearing that any effort to tinker with R&D systems might delay new-product introductions or dampen creativity, have only reluctantly applied it to them. In our experience, the meandering development timelines, bureaucratic roadblocks, and high levels of waste in the development processes of many companies do far more to dampen the spirits of top engineers than senior managers suspect. By seizing on the sense of urgency that difficult times create and challenging long-held assumptions about R&D processes, organizations can pinpoint the huge potential for improvement while sparking their employees' creativity and energy.

An aerospace company, for example, used the conversations that a value-stream mapping exercise[1] sparked to identify unnecessary process checks, wasteful approval requirements, and hidden bottlenecks in the flow of its R&D activities. Engineers found the exercise energizing and useful because it gave them their first opportunity to compare notes with other departments. It also initiated frank, fact-based discussions between engineers and senior managers about the causes of the bottlenecks and administrative delays that engineers observed in their day-to-day work. These discussions led to process changes that helped to increase the productivity of engineers involved in early-stage design activities by 25 percent. Such results aren't unusual. Indeed, when large manufacturers focus lean teams on R&D, the teams often identify improvements that raise productivity by an amount equivalent to 8 to 10 percent of a company's R&D costs while speeding time to market by up to 15 percent.

Related articles on mckinseyquarterly.com

From lean to lasting: Making operational improvements stick

When efficient capital and operations go hand in hand

Freeing up cash from operations

Finally, while some R&D units are instituting hiring freezes and mandatory reductions, forward-looking organizations are searching outside for specialist talent in hopes of stealing a march on competitors. Some companies we know are proactively weeding out underperformers. A McKinsey study of the IT and business process outsourcing sectors found that top-quartile engineers were more than twice as productive as those in the bottom quartile,[2] so a company that makes such moves can capture big savings quickly.

Notably, a few companies we know have explored their cost-management opportunities by redeploying talented engineers freed up through portfolio reviews. One automaker rotated some engineers into small, short-term projects, where—supported by functional experts such as purchasers and marketers—they looked for innovative, cost-saving ways to change products. These teams generated ideas, expected to be worth $2 billion a year, for modifying features, applying existing technology to new applications, and negotiating with suppliers for lower prices. What's more, a few high-tech companies are capitalizing on the closer links between engineers and marketers to take a deep look at how much value consumers place on specific product features. One consumer electronics company, for example, used this information to modify a key product and reposition it into a higher-value consumer segment, ultimately increasing its gross margins by 30 percent. Q

The authors wish to thank Ashish Kothari and Christopher Schorling for their help with this article.

[1] A lean-management technique used to examine the flow of information and materials needed to bring a product to market.

[2] In some cases, the differences are much larger. Among software makers, for instance, we've observed productivity gaps, between top and bottom performers, that exceed a factor of ten.

High tech:
Finding opportunity in the downturn

In the past, high-tech companies that made these five kinds of moves emerged as leaders of the pack when the economy improved.

Andrew Cheung, Eric Kutcher, and Dilip Wagle

Andrew Cheung is an associate principal in McKinsey's Silicon Valley office, Eric Kutcher is a principal in the Stamford office, and Dilip Wagle is a principal in the Seattle office.

With the global economy in recession, retrenchment seems to be the favored course of action for many companies. Our research, however, suggests that conventional strategies may not serve the technology industry well. McKinsey analyzed the performance of nearly 700 companies during technology contractions in markets around the world over the past two decades. We found that the turmoil accompanying downturns significantly reconfigured the high-tech landscape, with about half of the companies that entered a downturn as leaders (the top 20 percent) ending up as laggards when the economy regained momentum. To better weather the recession, companies should begin by reflecting on the broader forces at work in their operating environment.

The dynamics and impact of the contraction

Revenue is declining and will continue to do so, yet the contours of the downturn will differ dramatically by subsector. Technology companies experience more severe volatility during downturns than other industries do. Spending on high-tech goods and services traditionally falls much further than it does in most other product categories. During the peak-to-trough of recessionary periods, the drop is two to seven times greater than that of real GDP growth (Exhibit 1). After the dot-com bubble burst in 2000, IT spending fell a precipitous 27 percent, compared with a 3.7 percent drop in GDP. At the beginning of the current downturn, IT spending was 3.05 percent of GDP, below the 3.3 percent average of the last ten years and well below the 2000 peak of 4.1 percent, suggesting this downturn could be toward the lower end of this range. However, some tech segments will feel the brunt of the slowdown more than others. Hardware—from laptops to component manufacturers—is likely to be hit much harder than security software or maintenance services, which are essential to keeping corporate IT departments running and where spending is less discretionary.

Be aware of how liquidity issues may affect operations
Relative to other industries, the credit flow for technology companies is stable and most companies have enough cash to service short-term debt. However, problems are mounting along the supply chain, particularly among distributors and contract manufacturers in overseas markets. These developments ultimately could affect many companies' operations (Exhibit 2). After reviewing 3,700 high-tech companies, we forecast that one in four will need to tap into a credit line or to refinance debt over the next year. In some subsectors—such as component manufacturing, distribution, and manufacturing services—up to 50 percent of companies will face the need for funding. The impact on contract manufacturers in Asia is already evident, as order flows become less predictable and the cost of funding operations from credit lines becomes prohibitive.

EXHIBIT 1

Tech tumble

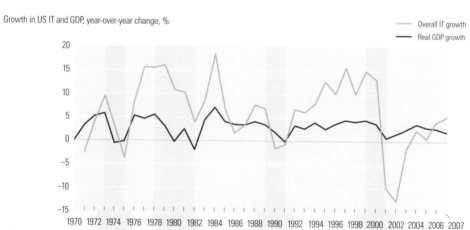

Source: Bureau of Economic Analysis; the *Economist*; IDC; McKinsey analysis

EXHIBIT 2

Liquid losses

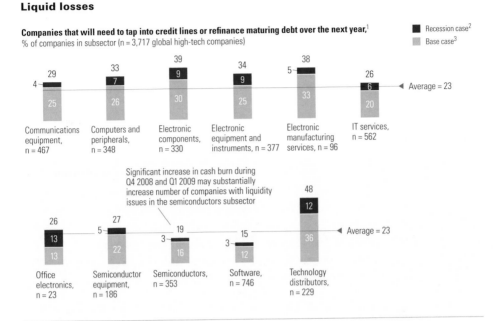

Companies that will need to tap into credit lines or refinance maturing debt over the next year,[1]
% of companies in subsector (n = 3,717 global high-tech companies)

■ Recession case[2]
■ Base case[3]

[1] Percent of companies within each subsector that have dynamic liquidity ratio (short-term debt divided by cash plus expected cash flow) of <100% and >0.
[2] Assumes decline in sales of −23.6% for hardware, −11.8% for software, and −14.8% for IT services; assumes costs of goods sold are variable, all other costs fixed.
[3] Base case reflects 2007 data.

Source: Bloomberg; McKinsey Global Institute analysis; McKinsey analysis

Understanding these broader macroeconomic forces and liquidity issues will help companies prepare a course of action. We took the above research further to better understand how tactical and strategic moves can affect tech companies' competitive standing after a downturn. We studied the performance of publicly traded high-tech companies across 12 subsectors around the world[1] during the period from 1995 to 2005, which encompasses the severe tech downturn of 2000–02. We ranked each of 688 companies by market-to-book value as well as return on invested capital (ROIC) and categorized them as leaders (those in the top 20 percent on both dimensions) or laggards (the remaining 80 percent). We then charted how their market positions changed over the course of the recession and into the recovery period (Exhibit 3). Our research suggests that the following decisive management moves, among others, can determine how well companies weather the downturn.

Optimize SG&A expenses and overall headcount

While controlling operating expenses is critical, leaders tended to treat expense categories differently. Leaders who maintained their positions increased sales, general, and administrative (SG&A) expenses by

[1] These companies had sales of more than $100 million in 1997 and 1998 and were publicly listed during the years from 1995 to 2005.

6 percent more in absolute dollar terms than leaders who fell from the top rung. These same companies actually increased overall head counts by 2 percent (compared with an 8 percent cut for those companies that dropped from the leadership ranks). For leaders, the growth in SG&A costs took place even as sales declined by 5 percent.

Related articles on mckinseyquarterly.com

Leading through uncertainty

Financial crises past and present

Managing IT spending

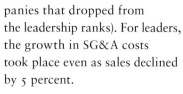

Make frequent, significant acquisitions and divestitures Companies that emerged as leaders used the downturn to make significant acquisitions that strengthened their product portfolio. A review of the 2000–02 recession shows that postrecession leaders were 30 percent more likely to make acquisitions and did so more frequently—racking up 26 percent more deals. They tended to wait until later in the downturn,

EXHIBIT 3

Trading places

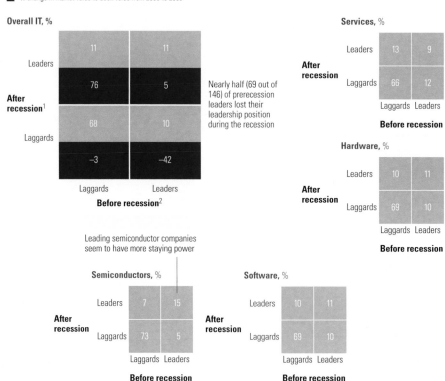

■ % of companies
■ % change in market value to book value from 2000 to 2003

Overall IT, %

	Laggards	Leaders
Leaders	11	11
	76	5
Laggards	68	10
	–3	–42

After recession[1]

Before recession[2]

Nearly half (69 out of 146) of prerecession leaders lost their leadership position during the recession

Services, %

After recession

	Laggards	Leaders
Leaders	13	9
Laggards	66	12

Before recession

Hardware, %

After recession

	Laggards	Leaders
Leaders	10	11
Laggards	69	10

Before recession

Leading semiconductor companies seem to have more staying power

Semiconductors, %

After recession

	Laggards	Leaders
Leaders	7	15
Laggards	73	5

Before recession

Software, %

After recession

	Laggards	Leaders
Leaders	10	11
Laggards	69	10

Before recession

[1]Based on 2004 and 2005.
[2]Based on 1998 and 1999.

Source: Standard & Poor's; McKinsey analysis

when targets' valuations were most attractive. Leaders also used the downturn to streamline the number of segments in which they operated. Postrecession leaders were 50 percent more likely to divest noncore businesses than laggards—a move that improved their overall positioning in the remaining businesses.

Maintain a stable leverage level relative to equity

Maintaining or improving the debt-to-equity (D/E) ratio throughout the recession was a hallmark of high-performing companies. While some leaders even managed to pay down debt, the distinguishing characteristic is that laggard companies increased their D/E ratio by 950 basis points on average (almost doubling their leverage). Given the steep drop in technology spending during contractions, such escalating debt loads leave these companies little room for investing in operational improvements, much less acquisitions or new product development. Particularly for the laggards, uncontrolled D/E leverage and heightened liquidity risk depress valuations just when market-to-book ratios of all but the leading firms are falling—as they generally do in downturns.

We welcome your comments on this article. Please send them to quarterly_comments@mckinsey.com.

Technology companies that take these actions may find improved opportunities to increase revenues through enhanced pricing power, the domination of a product segment, or the introduction of new products made possible by higher R&D spending. Q

The full version of this article is available on mckinseyquarterly.com.

The **irrational side** of change management

Most change programs fail, but the odds of success can be greatly improved by taking into account nine counterintuitive insights about how employees interpret their environment and choose to act.

**Carolyn Aiken and
Scott Keller**

In 1996, John Kotter published *Leading Change.* Considered by many to be the seminal work in the field of change management, Kotter's research revealed that only 30 percent of change programs succeed. Since the book's release, literally thousands of books and journal articles have been published on the topic, and courses dedicated to managing change are now part of many major MBA programs. Yet in 2008, a McKinsey survey of 3,199 executives around the world found, as Kotter did, that only one transformation in three succeeds. Other studies over the past ten years reveal remarkably similar results. It seems that, despite prolific output, the field of change management hasn't led to more successful change programs.

It also hasn't helped that most academics and practitioners now agree on the building blocks for influencing employee attitudes and management behavior. McKinsey's Emily Lawson and Colin Price provided a holistic perspective in "The psychology of change management,"[1] which suggests that four basic conditions are necessary before employees will change their behavior: a) *a compelling story*, because employees must see the point of the change and agree with it; b) *role modeling*, because they must also see the CEO and colleagues they admire behaving in the new way; c) *reinforcing mechanisms*, because systems, processes, and incentives must be in line with the new behavior; and d) *capability building*, because employees must have the skills required to make the desired changes.

Neil Webb

[1]Colin Price and Emily Lawson, "The psychology of change management," mckinseyquarterly.com, June 2003.

This prescription is well grounded in the field of psychology and is entirely rational. One of its merits is its intuitive appeal: many managers feel that, once revealed, it is simply good common sense. And this, we believe, is precisely where things go wrong. The prescription is right, but rational managers who attempt to put the four conditions in place by applying "common sense" typically misdirect time and energy, create messages that miss the mark, and experience frustrating unintended consequences from their efforts to influence change. Why? Because when they implement the prescription, they disregard certain, sometimes irrational—but predictable—elements of human nature.

In our research and by working with companies attempting change, we have identified nine insights into how human nature gets in the way of successfully applying the four conditions required for behavioral change. As we describe these insights, we'll show how various companies have, either by conscious awareness or simple luck, overcome or leveraged counterintuitive sides of human behavior in making change happen.

Creating a compelling story
Change-management thinking extols the virtues of creating a compelling change story, communicating it to employees, and following it up with ongoing communications and involvement. This is good advice, but in practice there are three pitfalls to achieving the desired impact.

1. What motivates you doesn't motivate most of your employees. We see two types of change stories consistently told in organizations. The first is the "good to great" story: something along the lines of, "Our historical advantage has been eroded by intense competition and changing customer needs; if we change, we can regain our leadership position." The second is the turnaround story: "We're performing below industry standard and must change dramatically to survive. We can become a top-quartile performer in our industry by exploiting our current assets and earning the right to grow."

These stories both seem intuitively rational, yet they too often fail to have the impact that change leaders desire. Research by a number of leading thinkers in the social sciences, such as Danah Zohar, has shown that when managers and employees are asked what motivates them the most in their work they are equally split among five forms of impact—impact on society (for instance, building the community and stewarding resources), impact on the customer (for example, providing superior service), impact on the company and its shareholders, impact on the working team (for example, creating a caring environment), and impact on "me" personally (my development, paycheck, and bonus).

This finding has profound implications for leaders. What the leader cares about (and typically bases at least 80 percent of his or her message to others on) does not tap into roughly 80 percent of the workforce's primary motivators for putting extra energy into the change program. Change leaders need to be able to tell a change story that covers all five things that motivate employees. In doing so, they can unleash tremendous amounts of energy that would otherwise remain latent in the organization.

Consider a cost reduction program at a large US financial-services company. The program started with a change story that ticked the conventional boxes related to the company's competitive position and future. Three months into the program, management was frustrated with employee resistance. The change team worked together to recast the story to include an element related to society (to deliver affordable housing, for example), customers (fewer errors, more competitive prices), the company (expenses are growing faster than revenues, which is not sustainable), working teams (less duplication, more delegation), and individuals (more attractive jobs).

This relatively simple shift in approach lifted employee motivation measures from 35.4 percent to 57.1 percent in a month, and the program went on to achieve 10 percent efficiency improvements in the first year—a run rate far above initial expectations.

2. You're better off letting them write their own story. Well-intentioned leaders invest significant time in communicating their change story. Road shows, town halls, and Web sites are but a few of the many approaches typically used. Certainly the story (told in five ways) needs to get out there, but the insight we are offering is that much of the energy invested in communicating it would be better spent listening, not telling.

In a famous behavioral experiment, half the participants are randomly assigned a lottery ticket number while the others are asked to write down any number they would like on a blank ticket. Just before drawing the winning number, the researchers offer to buy back the tickets from their holders. The result: no matter what geography or demographic environment the experiment has taken place in, researchers have always found that they have to pay at least five times more to those who came up with their own number.

This reveals something about human nature: when we choose for ourselves, we are far more committed to the outcome (almost by a factor of five to one). Conventional approaches to change management underestimate this impact. The rational thinker sees it as a waste of time to let others discover for themselves what he or she already knows—why not just tell them and be done with it? Unfortunately this approach steals from others the energy needed to drive change that comes through a sense of ownership of the answer.

At BP, to develop a comprehensive training program for frontline leaders, a decision was made to involve every key constituency in the design of the program, giving them a sense of "writing their own lottery ticket." It took a year and a half to complete the design using this model but was well worth it: now in implementation, the program is the highest rated of its kind at BP. More than 250 active senior managers from across the business willingly teach the course, and, most important, managers who have been through the training program are consistently ranked higher in performance than those who haven't, both by their bosses and by the employees who report to them.

3. It takes a story with both + and – to create real energy. The "deficit based" approach—which identifies the problem, analyzes what's wrong and how to fix it, plans, and then takes action—has become the model predominantly taught in business schools and is presumably the default change model in most organizations. Research has shown, however, that a story focused on what's wrong invokes blame and creates fatigue and resistance, doing little to engage people's passion and experience.

This has led to the rise of the "constructionist based" approach to change, where the change process is based on *discovery* (discovering the best of what is), *dreaming* (imagining what might be), *designing* (talking about what should be), and *destiny* (creating what will be). The problem with this approach is that an overemphasis on the positive can lead to watered-down aspirations and impact. The reason is that, as humans, we are more willing to take risks to avoid losing what we've got than we are to gain something more. Some anxiety is useful when it comes to spurring behavioral change.

The fact is that human beings consistently think they are better than they are—a phenomenon referred to in psychology as a **self-serving bias**

We believe the field of change management has drawn an artificial divide between deficit-based and constructionist-based approaches and stories. While it is impossible to prescribe generally how the divide should be split between positive and negative messages (as it will be specific to the context of any given change program), we strongly advise managers not to swing the pendulum too far in one direction or another. Consider Jack Welch, former CEO at GE, who took questions of "what's wrong here?" (poorly performing businesses, silo-driven behavior, and so forth) head-on, as well as "imagining what might be" (number one or two in every business, openness, and accountability).

Role modeling

Conventional change management suggests leaders should take actions that role model the desired change and mobilize a group of influence leaders to drive change deep into the organization. Unfortunately, this does not necessarily deliver the desired impact.

4. Leaders believe mistakenly that they already "are the change." Most senior executives understand and generally buy into Ghandi's famous aphorism, "Be the change you want to see in the world." They commit themselves to personally role modeling the desired behaviors. And then, in practice, nothing significant changes.

The reason for this is that most executives don't count themselves among the ones who need to change. How many executives when asked privately will say no to the question, "Are you customer focused?" and yes to the question "Are you a bureaucrat?" Of course, none. The fact is that human beings consistently think they are better than they are—a phenomenon referred to in psychology as a self-serving bias. Consider that 94 percent of men rank themselves in the top half according to male athletic ability. Whereas conventional change-management approaches surmise that top team role modeling is a matter of will or skill, the truth is that the real bottleneck to role modeling is knowing what to change at a personal level.

Typically, insight into what to change can be created by concrete 360-degree feedback techniques, either via surveys, conversations, or both. Look at Amgen CEO Kevin Sharer's approach of asking each of his top 75, "What should I do differently?" and then sharing his development needs and commitment publicly with them. Consider the top team of a national insurance company who routinely employed what they called the circle of fire during their change program: every participant receives feedback live—directly from their colleagues—in relation to being the change, such as "What makes you great?" and "What holds you back?"

5. "Influence leaders" aren't a panacea for making change happen. Almost all change-management literature places importance on identifying and mobilizing those in the organization who either by role or personality (or both) have disproportionate influence over how others think and behave. We believe this is sound and timeless advice. However, we have observed that the role of influence leaders has gradually shifted—from being perceived as a helpful element of a broader set of interventions, to a panacea for making change happen.

Our experiences working with change programs suggest that success depends less on how persuasive a few selected leaders are and more on how receptive the "society" is to the idea. In practice it is often unexpected members of the rank and file who feel compelled to step up and make a difference in driving change. That's why we warn against overinvesting in influence leaders and advocate that change leaders' attention should be balanced across the right application of all four conditions for change, to ensure they reinforce each other in ways that maximize the probability of the change spark taking off like wildfire across the organization.

Reinforcing mechanisms

Conventional change management emphasizes the importance of reinforcing and embedding desired changes in structures, processes, systems, target setting, and incentives. We agree. To be effective, however, these mechanisms must take into account that people don't always behave rationally.

6. Money is the most expensive way to motivate people. Companies that try to link the objectives of change programs to the compensation of staff find that it rarely enhances their motivation for change to the extent desired. The reason for this is as practical as it is psychological in nature. The reality is that in the vast majority of companies, it is exceedingly difficult to incorporate a meaningful link to the change program within compensation systems that are based on a vast array of metrics. Moreover, many studies have found that for human beings satisfaction equals perception minus expectation (an equation often accompanied by the commentary, "reality has nothing to do with it").

The beauty of this equation for change managers is that small, unexpected rewards can have disproportionate effects on employees' satisfaction with a change program. Gordon M. Bethune, while turning around Continental Airlines, sent an unexpected $65 check to every employee when Continental made it to the top five for on-time airlines. John McFarlane, former CEO of ANZ Bank, sent a bottle of champagne to every employee for Christmas with a card thanking them for their work on the company's "Perform, Grow, and Break-out" change program. Most change managers would refer to these as merely token gestures and argue that their impact is limited and short-lived. Employees on the receiving end beg to differ. Indeed, they consistently report back that the rewards have a disproportionately positive impact on change motivation that lasts for months, if not years.

7. The process and the outcome have got to be fair. Employees will go against their own self-interest if the situation violates other notions they have about fairness and justice. Consider a bank, which, as part of a major change program, created new risk-adjusted return on capital (RAROC) models and

delivered the resulting new pricing schedules to the front line along with new and appropriate sales incentives. The result: customer attrition (not only of the unprofitable ones) and price overrides went through the roof and significant value was destroyed by the effort. What went wrong? Because the frontline bankers perceived the changes as unfair to the customer, a significant number of them vocally bad-mouthed the bank's policies to customers and used price overrides to show their good faith, even though it meant they were less likely to achieve individual sales goals.

In making any changes to company structures, processes, systems, and incentives, change managers should pay what might strike them as an

Recommended reading

John P. Kotter, *Leading Change*, Boston: Harvard Business Press, 1996.

Danah Zohar, *Rewiring the Corporate Brain: Using the New Science to Rethink How We Structure and Lead Organizations*, San Francisco: Berrett-Koehler, 1997.

Richard Barrett, *Liberating the Corporate Soul: Building a Visionary Organization*, Woburn, MA: Butterworth-Heinemann, 1998.

Don Edward Beck and Christopher C. Cowan, *Spiral Dynamics: Mastering Values, Leadership, and Change*, Oxford, UK: Blackwell Publishing, 1996.

Ellen J. Langer, "The illusion of control," in *Judgment under Uncertainty: Heuristics and Biases*, eds. Daniel Kahneman, Paul Slovic, and Amos Tversky, Cambridge, UK: Cambridge University Press, 1982. This chapter describes the lottery ticket study mentioned on page 103.

Andreas Priestland and Robert Hanig, "Developing first-level leaders," *Harvard Business Review*, 2005, Volume 83, Number 6, pp. 112–20.

Bernard J. Mohr and Jane Magruder Watkins, *The Essentials of Appreciative Inquiry: A Roadmap for Creating Positive Futures*, Waltham, MA: Pegasus, 2002. The juxtaposition of the deficit-based and constructionist-based approaches to change is described in this work.

Daniel Kahneman and Amos Tversky, "Choices, values, and frames," *American Psychologist*, 1984, Volume 39, Number 4, pp. 341–50. In this article, Kahneman and Tversky propose evidence that humans are "irrational" loss avoiders.

Brad M. Barber and Terrance Odean, "Boys will be boys: Gender, overconfidence, and common stock investment," *Quarterly Journal of Economics*, 2001, Volume 116, Number 1, pp. 261–92.

Michael Ross and Fiore Sicoly, "Egocentric biases and availability and attribution," *Journal of Personality and Social Psychology*, 1979, Volume 37, pp. 322–36.

Dan Ariely, *Predictably Irrational: The Hidden Forces that Shape Our Decisions*, New York: Harper Collins, 2008.

Fred Nickols, "Change management books," home.att.net/~nickols/change_biblio.pdf, April 2, 2006. This list, compiled by Nickols, aggregates highly recommended books on change management.

unreasonable amount of attention to employees' sense of the fairness of the change process and its intended outcome. Particular care should be taken where changes affect how employees interact with one another (such as head count reductions and talent-management processes) and with customers (sales stimulation programs, call center redesigns, and pricing). Ironically, in the pricing example described above, the outcome was inherently fair (customers are being asked to pay commensurate to the risk the bank is taking on), and therefore the downward spiral described could have been avoided (and has been by other banks adopting RAROC-based pricing) by carefully tending to employees' perceptions of fairness in the communications and training surrounding the changes.

Capability building

Change-management literature emphasizes the importance of building the skills and talent needed for the desired change. Though hard to argue with, in practice there are two insights that demand attention in order to succeed.

8. Employees are what they think, feel, and believe in. As managers attempt to drive performance by changing the way employees behave, they all too often neglect the thoughts, feelings, and beliefs that, in turn, drive behavior. Consider a bank that through a benchmarking exercise discovered that its sales per banker were lagging behind those of the competition. After finding that bankers spent too little time with customers and too much time on paperwork, the bank set about reengineering the loan-origination process in order to maximize customer-facing time. Unfortunately, six months later, the levels of improvement were far lower than envisioned.

Related articles on mckinseyquarterly.com

The psychology of change management

Driving radical change

Creating organizational transformations: McKinsey Global Survey Results

A further investigation, with an eye to the bankers' mind-sets rather than their behaviors, revealed that they simply found customer interactions uncomfortable and therefore preferred paperwork. This feeling was driven by a combination of introverted personalities, poor interpersonal skills, and a feeling of inferiority when dealing with customers who (by and large) have more money and education than the bankers do. Finally, most bankers were loath to think of themselves as salespeople—a notion they perceived as better suited to employees on used-car lots than in bank branches.

Armed with these root-cause insights, training for bankers was expanded to include elements related to personality types, emotional intelligence, and vocational identity (recasting "sales" as the more noble pursuit of "helping customers discover and fulfill their unarticulated needs"). This enhancement not only put the program back on track within six months but also ultimately delivered sustainable sales lifts in excess of original targets.

9. Good intentions aren't enough. Good skill-building programs usually take into account that people learn better by doing than by listening. These programs are replete with interactive simulations and role plays, and commitments are made by participants regarding what they will "practice" back in the workplace. But come Monday morning, very few keep their commitments.

This lack of follow-through is usually not due to ill intent: it is because nothing formal has been done to lower the barriers to practicing new skills. The time and energy required to do something additional, or even to do something in a new way, simply don't exist in the busy day-to-day schedules of most employees. This failure to create the space for practice back in the workplace dooms most training programs to deliver returns that are far below their potential.

We advocate a number of enhancements to traditional training approaches in order to hardwire day-to-day practice into capability-building processes. First, training should not be a one-off event. Instead, a "field and forum" approach should be taken, in which classroom training is spread over a series of learning forums and fieldwork is assigned in between. Second, we suggest creating fieldwork assignments that link directly to the day jobs of participants, requiring them to put into practice new mind-sets and skills in ways that are hardwired into their responsibilities. These assignments should have quantifiable, outcome-based measures that indicate levels of competence gained and certification that recognizes and rewards the skills attained.

In the same way that the field of economics has been transformed by an understanding of uniquely human social, cognitive, and emotional biases, so too is the practice of change management in need of a transformation through an improved understanding of how humans interpret their environment and choose to act. While sustained impact can be measured only over numbers of years, our early results when applying these insights give us the confidence to broadly share our thinking. Q

Carolyn Aiken is a principal in McKinsey's Toronto office, and **Scott Keller** is a principal in the Chicago office. Copyright © 2009 McKinsey & Company. All rights reserved.

We welcome your comments on this article.
Please send them to quarterly_comments@mckinsey.com.

A Chinese view of governance and the financial crisis:
An interview with ICBC's chairman

Jiang Jianqing discusses the need for balance within an effective governance model and the ways the financial-services industry will change in China in the wake of the global economic crisis.

Dominic Barton, Yi Wang, and Mei Ye

Regulators struggling to fix the world's troubled financial institutions may take heart from the experience of China's large state-owned banks. In the late 1990s, Chinese state lenders were all but insolvent, with nonperforming loan ratios at many banks exceeding 50 percent. A decade later, China's state banks have found their footing—and have managed to keep it amid a global financial crisis that has their European and US counterparts reeling. The bad-loan ratio has been reduced, and this year China's state banks expect solid profits and continued rapid growth—despite the global downturn. What's more, top bank executives express confidence in their capacity to heed government instructions to boost lending while effectively controlling credit risk.

Industrial and Commercial Bank of China (ICBC) is generally regarded as the strongest of China's state-owned bank giants. It is also the largest bank by market capitalization and total profits—both in China and the world—with total assets of more than $1.4 trillion. ICBC chairman Jiang Jianqing met recently with McKinsey's Dominic Barton, Yi Wang, and Mei Ye to share his thoughts on corporate governance, risk management, and the origins of the financial crisis.

Jon Krause

The *Quarterly*: *Why has ICBC put so much effort into thinking about corporate governance?*

Jiang Jianqing: We share the vision of the Basel Committee[1] that good governance is essential not only for the stability of the banking industry but also for the economy as a whole. Effective governance is the means of building and maintaining the qualities that are at the foundation of all commerce: confidence and public trust. It's disheartening to see how many financial institutions lost sight of these basic truths. I find it ironic that some of the financial institutions that have struggled or even collapsed in wake of the financial crisis were touted as global role models before the crisis struck.

[1] An advisory panel including representatives from some of the world's leading central banks.

Jiang Jianqing

Vital statistics
Born February 1953, in Shanghai

Married, with 1 child

Education
Graduated with degree in finance and economics in 1984 from Shanghai University of Finance and Economics

Earned MA (1995) in engineering and PhD (1999) in management from Shanghai Jiao Tong University

Career highlights
Industrial and Commercial Bank of China (ICBC)
• Chairman and executive director (2005–present)
• President (2000–05)
• Vice president (1999–2000)
• President, Shanghai branch (1997–99)
• Vice president, Shanghai branch (1993–95)

ICBC (Asia)
• Chairman (2000–present)

Shanghai Municipal Cooperation Bank (now Bank of Shanghai)
• President (1995–97)

Fast facts
Vice president of the China Banking Association and the China Society for Finance and Banking

Senior faculty fellow and PhD supervisor, Shanghai Jiao Tong University

Has written for more than 20 publications

Distinguished Performance Award for Global Leadership by *Committee for Economic Development* (2008)

Named one of China's 25 most effective entrepreneur leaders by *China Entrepreneur Magazine* (2007 and 2008)

Leadership Achievement Award by *The Asian Banker* (2006)

I remember the findings of a 2002 McKinsey survey[2] concluding that institutional investors will pay a premium for stock offered by well-governed companies, especially in developing markets. The survey also found that, in deciding where to put their money in these countries, investors pay more attention to governance issues than to financial metrics. We recognize that corporate governance is an important tool for maximizing shareholder value, and that's why we put so much effort into thinking about it.

The *Quarterly*: *What lessons have you drawn about governance in the wake of the financial crisis?*

Jiang Jianqing: My view is that there is no single model of effective governance. What works in some countries or cultures may not work elsewhere. In the United States and Europe, equity investment is highly fragmented, so management of the company must be delegated to a board or a small number of key executives, and various incentive mechanisms must be used to motivate people at the helm to run the company in a way that creates value.

Many Asian businesses are controlled by a single family. Family-run firms are thought to be highly efficient. But regulating the relationship between large and small shareholders is often a problem. In China, large banks and businesses favor a model in which the state owns a large proportion of company shares. In our case, for example, Central Huijin Investment and China's Ministry of Finance each hold more than 30 percent of ICBC shares. Such arrangements aren't unique to China: in Austria, Israel, Singapore, and many other nations, the proportion of state ownership for large companies can range from 40 percent to 70 percent. The challenge with this model is how to manage complex networks of trust agency relationships. In these types of organizations, reliance on incentive systems alone tends to do more harm than good.

Each model has its strengths and weaknesses. They all bear careful study. It seems to me there are no obvious best practices. But we've learned from the financial crisis that there are plenty of *worst* practices.

Running a bank is like running a marathon: getting a fast start doesn't assure success. Indeed, runners in the lead after the first 1,000 meters may not even make it to the finish line. In a marathon, the key to victory is stamina and a balanced pace. Similarly, balance is the secret to effective governance. More specifically, what I mean by this is you have to balance

[2] See "Global Investor Opinion Survey," July 2002, mckinsey.com.

short- and long-term profits, as well as short- and long-term risks. I'm certainly not suggesting the Chinese approach to corporate governance is perfectly developed. But I do think there are flaws in the Western system of relying so heavily on incentive systems.

The *Quarterly*: *How do you control risk in a big institution like ICBC and how do you build that into the culture of the organization?*

Jiang Jianqing: We've learned our lessons on risk. In June 1999, the nonperforming loan ratio at ICBC reached 47.5 percent. At the time, some Western media claimed Chinese banks were technically bankrupt. You can't imagine the pressure we bankers faced then.

The first step in addressing the problem was to focus on risk management. After I was appointed president[3] in 2000, one of the first things I decided was that we must hold the nonperforming ratio for new loans to less than 2 percent of assets. We created a credit-management system to control existing and new loans. By addressing irregularities and punishing violators, the quality of new loans quickly improved. Since then, ICBC has kept its nonperforming ratio for new loans to 1.7 percent.

Changes in the regulatory environment helped as well. In the wake of the Asian financial crisis, the Chinese government reorganized and developed the nation's financial regulatory system, putting great emphasis on risk management, creating the China Banking Regulatory Commission, enacting a range of new rules and regulations, and introducing stricter external auditing and accounting standards. China's large commercial banks developed sound governance structures and were subjected to close scrutiny from investors as they prepared to list shares publicly. This combination of internal and external factors substantially improved the governance of China's financial institutions and left them in much better shape to manage risk today. Now ICBC's bad loan ratio has been reduced to 2.2 percent.

[3] Jiang became chairman of ICBC in 2005.

In the end, though, the key to risk control is employing good people. That's why we put so much emphasis on ethics and developing a corporate culture that values precision, professionalism, and teamwork. Good governance is impossible without a good corporate culture.

The *Quarterly*: *In response to the global financial crisis, the Chinese government has recently announced a series of measures to spur domestic demand. How do you balance concerns about maintaining credit quality with the bank's social responsibilities and government directives to support growth?*

Jiang Jianqing: The government's recent decision to boost domestic demand offers a great opportunity for the banking industry. However, ICBC is a commercial bank and we have to view these opportunities from the business perspective. I believe we have the ability to seize the opportunity and spur economic growth while also controlling risks. The fact that China's finance industry has not been badly hit by the ongoing crisis should be attributed to great efforts and timely reform initiated by the Chinese government after the Asian financial crisis. The high-risk situation that China's banking institutions experienced before is the last thing we want to see this time.

*'We shouldn't reject the need for innovation in financial services merely because it carries some **element of risk** with it'*

The *Quarterly*: *Has the financial crisis altered your thinking about the merits of introducing more complicated forms of financial products, such as credit default swaps or other derivatives?*

Jiang Jianqing: Derivatives weren't the straw that broke the camel's back. The current crisis is the result of a combination of problems. We shouldn't reject the need for innovation in financial services merely because it carries some element of risk with it. In China, we say: you can't stop eating just because you're afraid of choking on your food.

China's challenges differ from those faced by financial institutions in more developed economies. We haven't suffered severe losses in the current crisis, because we didn't invest in the complicated products that triggered it. But if you think carefully, this could be exactly where challenges emerge in the days to come. As interest rates are increasingly determined by the market and financial disintermediation that develops in China, the traditional loan-led banking model is bound to change. We'll have to have more complicated financial products. Yes, we need to minimize risk, but we can't dispense with innovation. The question is how to strike the proper balance. China's banking industry will suffer setbacks. The best we can hope is to limit the pain of adjustment.

The Quarterly: Could you talk a bit about your board? What do you expect your board to do to help you?

Jiang Jianqing: It is currently composed of 15 directors—4 executive directors, 7 nonexecutive directors, and 4 independent directors. I see the board as the soul of a company. Sound corporate governance has a lot to do with a board's structure, decision making style, and efficiency. The quality of a board's members determines the board's ability to perform its duties. A good board structure should be independent, professional, ethical, honest, and dedicated.

Related articles on mckinseyquarterly.com

Governing China's boards: An interview with John Thornton

Global investment strategies for China's financial institutions

Improving board performance in emerging markets

Our board has made great efforts to enhance ICBC's development and risk management. Shortly after the company went public, the board developed a three-year plan with specific targets around restructuring, regional development, innovation, differentiated service, cross-border operations, comprehensive risk management, IT, and HR. In the past three years, those targets have all been met or exceeded. These efforts have earned us global recognition. Last year, *The Banker* magazine picked ICBC as its "Bank of the Year" for Asia. We also were honored for excellence in corporate governance by the Chamber of Hong Kong Listed Companies.

The Quarterly: What are your goals for the bank in the years ahead?

Jiang Jianqing: Recently we designed the strategy for 2009 to 2011. We resolved that we will become the world's most profitable, preeminent, and respected bank.

Given our size, we feel we should be able to earn larger profits than any other bank. We seek rates of ROE,[4] ROA,[5] and income per customer on par with the highest levels in China and overseas. Since the introduction of international auditing, in 2003, we've enjoyed a CAGR[6] of 37.5 percent

[4] Return on equity.
[5] Return on assets.
[6] Compound annual growth rate.

in profits—making us one of the fastest-growing banks in the world. Our goal is to extend this cycle of profitability and rapid growth. We've set high standards of excellence for corporate governance, customer service, and financial innovation. We also aspire to be a global leader in the financial-services industry—with a strong brand name and a solid record for corporate citizenship and social responsibility.

The *Quarterly*: *What are your plans for international expansion?*

Jiang Jianqing: We're very cautious when it comes to investing. Before the crisis, we had many opportunities for acquisition. Fortunately we resisted that temptation. We have a clearly defined strategy. Any potential acquisition target must expand our regional footprint and improve ICBC's core competencies and long-term returns. So our overseas expansion will be a gradual process—another marathon. Q

Dominic Barton is a director in McKinsey's Shanghai office, where **Yi Wang** is a principal and **Mei Ye** is a consultant. Copyright © 2009 McKinsey & Company. All rights reserved.

By Invitation:
Insights and opinion from outside contributors

119   **Amar Bhidé** is the Lawrence D. Glaubinger Professor of Business at Columbia University.

Where innovation creates value

126   **Hayagreeva Rao** is the Atholl McBean Professor of Organizational Behavior and Human Resources in the Graduate School of Business at Stanford University.

Market rebels and radical innovation

It doesn't matter where scientific discoveries and breakthrough technologies originate—for national prosperity, the important thing is who commercializes them. The United States is not behind in that race.

Where innovation creates value

Amar Bhidé

Now, perhaps, more than ever, the fear of globalization haunts the United States. Many manufacturing companies that once flourished there fell to overseas competition or relocated much of their work abroad. Then services embarked on the same journey. Just as the manufacturing exodus started with low-wage, unskilled labor, the offshoring of services at first involved data entry, routine software programming and testing, and the operation of phone banks. But today, overseas workers analyze financial statements, test trading strategies, and design computer chips and software architectures for US companies.

It is the offshoring of research and development—of innovation and the future—that arouses the keenest anxiety. The economist Richard Freeman spoke for many Americans when he warned that the United States could become significantly less competitive "as large developing countries like China and India harness their growing scientific and engineering expertise to their enormous, low-wage labor forces."[1] What is the appropriate response? One, from the conservative pundit Pat Buchanan, the TV broadcaster Lou Dobbs, and their like, calls for protectionism. Another, seemingly more progressive, approach would be to spend more money to promote cutting-edge science and technology. Much of the establishment, Democratic and Republican alike, has embraced what the economists Sylvia Ostry and Richard Nelson call techno-nationalism and techno-fetishism, which both claim that US prosperity requires continued domination of these fields.

[1] See Ashley Pettus, "Overseas insourcing," *Harvard Magazine*, 2005, Volume 108, Number 2.

We've heard such fears and prescriptions before. In the 1980s, many people attributed the problems of the US economy to the proliferation of lawyers and managers and to a shortage of engineers and scientists; Japan and Germany were praised as countries with a better occupational ratio. Yet in the 1990s, their economies slackened while the United States prospered—and not because it heeded the warnings. Indeed, math and science education in US high schools didn't improve much. Enrollment in law schools remained high, and managers accounted for a growing proportion of the workforce. The US share of scientific articles, science and engineering PhDs, and patents continued to decline, the service sector to expand, and manufacturing employment to stagnate.

Of course, the United States can't count on the same happy ending to every episode of the "losing our lead" serial. The integration of China and India into the global economy is a seminal and unprecedented phenomenon. Could the outcome be different this time? Is the United States on the verge of being pummeled by a technological hurricane? In my view, the answer is no. Worries about the offshoring of R&D and the progress of science in China and India arise from a failure to understand technological innovation and its relation to the global economy. Innovation does play a major role in nurturing prosperity, but we must be careful to formulate policies that sustain rather than undermine it—for instance, by favoring one form of innovation over another.

Three levels of innovation
Innovation involves the development of new products or processes and the know-how that begets them. New products can take the form of high-level building blocks or raw materials (for example, microprocessors or the silicon of which they are made), midlevel intermediate goods (motherboards with components such as microprocessors), and ground-level final products (such as computers). Similarly, the underlying know-how for new products includes high-level general principles, midlevel technologies, and ground-level, context-specific rules of thumb. For microprocessors, this know-how includes the laws of solid-state physics (high level), circuit designs and chip layouts (midlevel), and the tweaking of conditions in semiconductor fabrication plants to maximize yields and quality (ground level).

Technological innovations, especially high-level ones, usually have limited economic or commercial importance unless complemented by lower-level innovations. Breakthroughs in solid-state physics, for example, have value for the semiconductor industry only if accompanied by new microprocessor designs, which themselves may be largely useless without plant-level tweaks that make it possible to produce these components in large quantities. A new microprocessor's value may be impossible to realize without new motherboards and computers, as well.

New know-how and products also require interconnected, nontechnological innovations on a number of levels. A new diskless (thin-client) computer, for instance, generates revenue for its producer and value for its users only if it is marketed effectively and deployed properly. Marketing and organizational innovations are usually needed; for example, such a computer may force its manufacturer to develop a new sales pitch and materials and its users to reorganize their IT departments.

Arguing about which innovations or innovators make the greatest contribution to economic prosperity, however, isn't helpful, for they all play necessary and complementary roles. Innovations that sustain prosperity are developed and used in a huge game involving many players working on many levels over many years.

Consider, for instance, the story of the key active component in almost all modern electronics: the transistor. A pair of German physicists obtained the first patents for it in the 1920s and '30s. In 1947, William Shockley and two colleagues at Bell Labs built the first practical point-contact transistor, which Bell used only in small quantities. In 1950, Shockley developed the radically different bipolar junction transistor, licensed to companies such as Texas Instruments, which at first implemented it in a limited run of radios that were used as a sales tool. Within two decades, transistors had replaced vacuum tubes in radios and TVs and spawned a whole world of new devices, such as electronic calculators and personal computers.

The German physicists' discoveries began an extended process of developing know-how at a number of levels. Some steps involved high-level discoveries, such as the transistor effect, which earned Shockley and his colleagues a Nobel Prize. Other steps, such as those needed to obtain high production yields in semi-

conductor plants, called for lower-level, context-specific knowledge.

A similar complexity characterizes globalization. A variety of cross-border flows can be important to innovators—for instance, the diffusion of scientific principles and technological breakthroughs, the licensing of know-how, the export and import of final products, the procurement of intermediate goods and services (offshoring), equity investments, and the use of immigrant labor. Many kinds of global interactions have become more common, but not in a uniform way: international trade in manufactured goods has soared, but most services remain untraded. Of the many activities in the innovation game, only some are performed well in remote, low-cost locations; many midlevel activities, for example, are best conducted close to potential customers.

Where technomania goes wrong
Techno-nationalists and techno-fetishists oversimplify innovation by equating it with discoveries announced in scientific journals and with patents for cutting-edge technologies developed in university or commercial research labs. Since they rarely distinguish between the different levels and kinds of know-how, they ignore the contributions of the other players—contributions that don't generate publications or patents.

They oversimplify globalization as well—for example, by assuming that high-level ideas and know-how rarely if ever cross national borders and that only the final products made with it are traded. Actually, ideas and technologies move from country to country quite easily, but much final output, especially in the service sector, does not. The findings of science are available—for the price of learned books and journals—to any country that can use them. Advanced technology, by contrast, does have commercial value because it can be patented, but patent owners generally don't charge higher fees to foreigners. In the early 1950s, what was then a tiny Japanese company called Sony was among the first licensors of Bell Labs' transistor patent, for $50,000.

In a world where breakthroughs travel easily, their national origins are fundamentally unimportant. Notwithstanding the celebrated claim of the author and *New York Times* columnist Thomas Friedman, it *doesn't* matter that Google's search algorithm was developed in California. An Englishman invented the World Wide Web's protocols in a Swiss lab. A Swede and a Dane started Skype, the leading provider of peer-to-peer Internet telephony, in Estonia. To be sure, the foreign provenance of such advances does not harm the US economy (see sidebar, "Innovation in health care").

What is true for breakthroughs from Switzerland, Sweden, Denmark, and Estonia is true as well for those from China, India, and other emerging economies. We should expect—and desire—that as prosperity spreads, more places will contribute to humanity's stock of scientific and technological knowledge. The nations of the earth are not locked into a winner-take-all race for leadership in these fields: the enhancement of research capabilities in China and India, and thus their share of cutting-edge work, will improve living standards

in the United States, which, if anything, should encourage these developments rather than waste valuable resources fighting them.

The willingness and ability of lower-level players to create new know-how and products is at least as important to an economy as the scientific and technological breakthroughs on which they rest. Without radio manufacturers such as Sony, for instance, transistors might have remained mere curiosities in a lab. Maryland has a higher per capita income than Mississippi not because Maryland is or was an extremely significant developer of breakthrough technologies but because of its greater ability to benefit from them. Conversely, the city of Rochester, New York—home to Kodak and Xerox—is reputed to have one of the highest per capita levels of patents of all US cities. It is far from the most economically vibrant among them, however.

More than 40 years ago, the British economists Charles Carter and Bruce Williams warned that "it is easy to impede [economic] growth by excessive research, by having too high a percentage of scientific manpower engaged in adding to the stock of knowledge and too small a percentage engaged in using it. This is the position in Britain today."[2] It is very much to the point that the United States has not only great scientists and research labs but also many players that can exploit high-level breakthroughs regardless of where they originate. An increase in the supply of high-level know-how, no matter

[2] Charles F. Carter and Bruce R. Williams, "Government scientific policy and the growth of the British economy," *The Manchester School*, 1964, Volume 32, Number 3, pp. 197–214.

what its source, provides more raw material for mid- and ground-level innovations that raise US living standards.

Techno-fetishism and techno-nationalism also ignore the implications of the service sector's ever-growing share of the US economy. Manufacturing, with just 12 percent of US GDP, accounts for some 42 percent of the country's R&D and employs a disproportionately large number of its scientists, technicians, and engineers. Services, with about 70 percent of US GDP, accounts

Innovation in health care

The medical sector illustrates the high-level bias of public policy, as well as the large potential benefits of focusing more on the development and use of mid- and ground-level innovations. The United States spends more of its national income on health care—about 16 percent of GDP—than any other country. Yet in many ways it isn't getting value for money.[1] In 2007, 40 countries had lower infant mortality rates and 44 higher life expectancy.

Skimpy government support for high-level medical research certainly isn't the problem. On the contrary, from 1998 to 2003 government funding for health care R&D, as a proportion of 2004 GDP, was more than ten times higher in the United States than in Austria, Sweden, or Switzerland—which had lower infant mortality rates and higher life expectancy. And government-funded research is far from the whole story: foundations and for-profit companies put up much more money than the tax-funded National Institutes of Health does.

Yet some people in the United States worry that China and India threaten US preeminence in basic medical research. In February 2006, for example, Business Week warned that China's State Council had substantially increased R&D funding, with biotechnology at the top of the list. The story highlights an experimental gene therapy, for treating cancers, in which the country was ominously said to be "racing to a lead."[2] How would US health care or economic prosperity suffer if Chinese government subsidies made it possible to cure more cancers? An obsession with staying ahead in every possible frontier of medical research diverts money and attention from health services reform, which would provide far greater payoffs that would remain largely in the United States. Some experts advocate a broader role for the government in fixing the system's troubles, others a more market-oriented approach. But almost all experts agree that the solution isn't more or better medical research—it's changing the game so that hospitals will be better managed, IT used more widely and effectively, and insurance schemes better organized.

In the effort to reform health care services, innovative entrepreneurs could play an important role, if they were allowed to do so. Although they have improved productivity in just about every other sector of the US economy, in the "bloated, inefficient health care system," as Harvard's Regina Herzlinger observes, innovation has been restricted to medical technologies and health insurance. Entrepreneurs have difficulty attempting to provide care at lower cost—the heart of any real solution—because "status quo providers, abetted by legislators and insurance companies, have made it virtually impossible for them to succeed."[3]

[1] See Diana Farrell, Eric S. Jensen, and Bob Kocher, "Why Americans pay more for health care," in this issue.
[2] Bruce Einhorn, "A cancer treatment you can't get here," *Business Week*, March 6, 2006.
[3] Regina Herzlinger, *Who Killed Health Care? America's $2 Trillion Medical Problem—and the Consumer-Driven Cure*, New York, NY: McGraw Hill, 2007.

for a disproportionately low one. But this doesn't mean that the service sector shuns innovation. As the economist Dirk Pilat notes, "R&D in services is often different in character from R&D in manufacturing. It is less oriented toward technological developments and more at codevelopment, with hardware and software suppliers, of ways to apply technology" to products.[3] Whatever proportion of resources a manufacturing economy should devote to formal research (or research labs) and to educating scientists, the appropriate proportion would be lower in a services-based economy.

Consider a particularly important aspect of the US service sector: its use of innovations in information technology. It simply doesn't matter where they were developed; the benefits accrue mainly to US workers and consumers because, in contrast to manufacturing, most services generated in the United States are consumed there. Suppose that IT researchers in, say, Germany create an application that helps retailers to cut inventories. Wal-Mart Stores and many of its US competitors have shown conclusively that they are much more likely to use such technologies than retailers in, for example, Germany, where regulations and a preference for picturesque but inefficient small-scale shops discourage companies from taking a chance on anything new. That is among the main reasons why since the mid-1990s, productivity and incomes have grown faster in the United States than in Europe and Japan.

Changing course

Since innovation is not a zero-sum game among nations, and high-level science and engineering are no more important than the ability to use them in mid- and ground-level innovations, the United States should reverse policies that favor the one over the other, and it should cease to worry that the forward march of the rest of the human race will reduce it to ruin.

One obvious example of its mistaken policies is the provision of subsidies and grants for R&D but not for the marketing of products or for the development of ground-level know-how to help the people who use them. Similarly, companies such as Wal-Mart have very large IT budgets and staffs that develop a great deal of ground-level expertise and even develop in-house systems. But none of this qualifies for R&D incentives.

Policies to promote long-term investment by providing tax credits for capital equipment and for brick-and-mortar structures seem outdated as well. The purchase price of enterprise-resource-planning systems, for example, is just a fraction of the total cost of the projects to implement them. Yet businesses eligible for investment-tax credits to buy computer hardware or software don't receive tax breaks for the cost of training users, adapting hardware and software systems to the specific needs of a company, or reengineering its business processes to accommodate them.

Immigration policies that favor high-level research by preferring highly trained engineers and scientists to people who hold only bachelor's

---

[3] Dirk Pilat, "Innovation and productivity in services: State of the art," Organisation for Economic Co-operation and Development, 2001.

degrees are misguided too. By working in, say, the IT departments of retailers and banks, immigrants who don't have advanced degrees probably make as great a contribution to the US economy as those who do. Likewise, the US patent system is excessively attuned to the needs of R&D labs and not enough to those of innovators developing mid- and ground-level products, which often don't generate patentable intellectual property under current rules and are often threatened by easily obtained high-level patents.

Thomas Friedman to the contrary, the world is hardly flat: China and India aren't close to catching up with the United States in the ability to develop and use technological innovations. Starting afresh may allow these countries to leapfrog ahead in some respects—building advanced mobile-phone networks, for example. But excelling in the overall innovation game requires a great and diverse team, which takes a very long time to build.

Japan, for instance, began to modernize itself in the late 1860s. Within a few decades, it had utterly transformed its industry, educational system, and military. Today, the country's highly developed economy makes important contributions to technological progress. Yet after nearly 150 years of modernization, Japan remains behind the United States in the overall capacity to develop and use those innovations, as average productivity data

show. South Korea and Taiwan, which have enjoyed truly miraculous growth rates since the 1970s, are still further behind. Do China and India have any real likelihood, at any time in the foreseeable future, of attaining the parity with the United States that has so far eluded Japan, South Korea, and Taiwan?

Complacency is dangerous, but fretting over imaginary threats impairs the ability to address real ones. A misguided fear of scientific and technological progress in China and India distracts Americans both from its benefits and from the important problems created by the integration of these two countries into the global economy—such as the soaring per capita fossil fuel consumption of more than two billion people. We do have much to worry about. Let's worry about the right things. Q

This article summarizes the first and last chapters of Amar Bhidé's book *The Venturesome Economy: How Innovation Sustains Prosperity in a More Connected World* (New Jersey: Princeton University Press, 2008). Copyright © 2009 McKinsey & Company. All rights reserved.

We welcome your comments on this article. Please send them to quarterly_comments@ mckinsey.com.

Activists play a key role in making or breaking new markets, products, and services. Managers who think like insurgents can shape market acceptance of innovations while stimulating radical change within the organization.

Market rebels and radical innovation

Hayagreeva Rao

Activists who challenge the status quo play a critical but often overlooked role in both promoting and impeding radical business innovation. Their importance stems from the very nature of innovation, which frequently challenges existing interests, norms, values, social practices, and relationships. As a result, the joined hands of market rebels—activists and their recruits—have with surprising frequency exerted significant influence on market acceptance of breakthrough products and services.

For example, nearly all of the technical aspects associated with personal computing were available by 1972, but the PC didn't take off until a few years later when hobbyists, rebelling against centralized computing, organized groups such as the Homebrew Computer Club. These clubs were spawning grounds for actors—such as inventors, founders of companies like Apple, and developers of programs and games—who collectively established the market for personal computers and eventually stimulated the entry of larger companies. Similarly, the hybrid car succeeded partly because market rebels in the environmental movement paved the way by arousing collective enthusiasm for "green" causes among consumers and regulators.

By contrast, radical innovations (such as the Segway personal transporter) have often floundered because their developers overlooked the social and cultural mobilization needed to excite their targeted consumers. More striking, the deaf rights movement slowed adoption of the cochlear implant—thought of by its makers as a cure for deafness because children who used it could more easily acquire language skills—by painting it as an innovation that presaged the loss of sign language and the destruction of the deaf community. In France, for example, a deaf coalition called *Sourds en Colère* (Deaf Anger) organized demonstrations against doctors who promoted cochlear implants.

These examples and many others hold valuable lessons for executives pursuing innovation. The costs to consumers of adopting such innovations are high because adopters have to topple existing conventions. Stimulating collective endeavors that initiate social change can be a critical part of reshaping markets.

To do so, companies must understand how market rebels forge a collective identity and mobilize support. Crucial for many activists is articulating a "hot cause," which arouses emotion and creates a community of members, and relying on "cool mobilization," which signals the identity of community members while sustaining their commitment. Companies also can boost their odds of harnessing the power of collective action by employing the right tactics, such as emphasizing two-way communication with consumers. Above all, a mind-set shift is needed: managers hoping to foster and encourage the diffusion of radical innovation need to start thinking like insurgents.

Hot causes and cool mobilization

Activists face a conundrum: should one concentrate on changing beliefs first or modifying behavior first? Hot causes and cool mobilization help to address this issue. Hot causes mobilize passions and engender new beliefs, and cool mobilization triggers new behavior while allowing new beliefs to develop. Together, they foster the development

of new identities and the defense of old ones.

By hot causes I mean those that inspire feelings of pride or anger. These emotions can be critical for overcoming another important challenge activists face: arousing to action individuals who are usually busy, distracted, uninvolved, or apparently powerless—and therefore reluctant to invest time and energy. A classic example is the quality movement that transformed the American automobile industry in the 1980s. One could have expected quality improvements to be undertaken by companies as a result of normal profit incentives. However, American automobile producers overlooked quality and initially disregarded Japanese innovations concerning quality circles. It was only after a threat was named—the death of the American automobile industry—that quality activists were able to mobilize support for quality institutes and initiatives.

Like hot causes, cool mobilization activates emotion and enables the formation of new identities, but it does so by engaging audiences in new behaviors and experiences that are improvisational and insurgent. The origins of the word *cool* can be traced to jazz musicians revolting against the legacy of Louis Armstrong, who had become synonymous with "hot jazz." I use the word here to capture the insurgent and improvisational dimensions of the jazz of such rebels as Charlie Parker, Dizzy Gillespie, and Miles Davis. The key to cool mobilization is engaging audiences through collective experiences that generate communities of feeling, in which audience

Visit mckinseyquarterly.com to watch a video of Hayagreeva Rao explaining the role of activists in making or breaking innovations.

members don't just have their emotions roused but encounter what literary critic Raymond Williams has called "social experiences in solution." Consider the recycling movement, which seeks to promote sustainable use of resources and rests on the daily ritual of carefully segregating glass, plastic, and paper so they can be put to later use.

Together, hot causes and cool mobilization power collective action, and collective action creates or constrains markets. Hot causes intensify emotions and trigger new beliefs. Cool mobilization engages participants in new collective experiences that transform beliefs. Hot causes are highly defined, and their definitions give them emotional resonance. Cool mobilization is less clearly defined and requires conscious participation—indeed, participants have to "fill out" the experience through their actions and experimentation. Both underlie the formation of new identities.

In the personal-computing movement, the hot cause was the tyranny of the central computer; the sources of cool mobilization were hobbyist clubs and, arguably, the PC itself. In the deaf rights movement, the hot cause was the cochlear implant—billed as a tool of cultural genocide. The cool mobilization came from deaf rights groups that used unconventional techniques—such as performing mime skits depicting

French doctors performing operations on blood-covered children—to arouse public interest.

Market rebels in action

The joined hands of market rebels can make or break radical innovations by exploiting hot causes and cool mobilization in many of the markets that affect our daily lives. It's easy to forget as we drive cars, drink beer, and take medicine that these markets have been shaped by social movements.

Rebels in new markets: Cultural acceptance of the car

The car, a radical invention that promised to transform the experience of transportation, was an extremely hot cause. In 1895, when the automobile industry was just beginning, the gasoline-powered car was poorly understood, notoriously unreliable, and reviled by vigilante antispeeding organizations. Colonel Albert Pope, a bicycle manufacturer who went on to make electric cars, could not fathom why anyone would use gas-powered ones, asserting, "You can't get people to sit over an explosion." And a lawmaker in Massachusetts suggested that motorists fire Roman candles at approaching horse-drawn carriages to warn them of the arrival of the car.

Yet as early as 1906, commentator Frank Munsey noted that the "uncertain period of the automobile is now past. It is no longer a theme for jokers, and rarely do we hear the derisive expression, 'Get a horse.'" Henry Ford is widely regarded as the man who established the automobile industry by automating production and driving down prices so the car could reach the masses. But it wasn't until 1913 that Ford installed the moving assembly line in Highland Park, Michigan, to produce the Model T—long after the car became taken for granted. What's more, Ford benefited from laws licensing drivers and mandating speed limits—and he didn't lobby or otherwise agitate for those rules.

Ford didn't need to, because a social movement powered by automobile clubs comprising car enthusiasts played a central role in legitimating the automobile and presenting it as a modern solution to the problem of transportation. These enthusiasts (primarily doctors and other professionals) were rebels who flouted convention, abandoned the horse-drawn carriage for the automobile, and sought to popularize its use. Neither sponsored nor financed by car manufacturers, the clubs were both social in nature and focused on improving quality, shielding car owners from legal harassment, and promoting the construction of good roads. Club involvement enabled members to construct an identity built around a new consumer role. By 1901, 22 clubs had mushroomed in cities from Boston to Newark to Chicago.

In addition to working with state governments to draft laws licensing cars and mandating speed limits, automobile clubs organized reliability contests that pitted cars against one another in endurance, hill climbing, and fuel-economy runs. Each contest was widely viewed as a test that proved to audiences that the automobile was reliable. The first reliability contest was in 1895; by 1912 the contests were discontinued because organizers recognized that the automobile had become a social fact.

Even Henry Ford needed to win a race in order to achieve the transition from engineer to entrepreneur. In a celebrated 1901 race, Ford, then an upstart producer, defeated the better-established Alexander Winton. Ford's wife, Clara, later described the scene after Ford took the lead in a letter to her brother, Milton Bryant: "The people went wild. One man threw his hat up, and when it came down, he stamped on it. Another man had to hit his wife on the head to keep her from going off the handle. She stood up in her seat … screamed, 'I'd bet $50 on Ford if I had it.'" The public acclaim that Ford received enabled him to create the Ford Motor Company in 1903.

Rebels in established markets: Microbrewing

September 26, 1997, was a watershed day in the history of the modern brewing industry in America: the Institute of Brewing Studies announced that the number of breweries in the United States exceeded those in Germany. In comparison to the 1,234 breweries in Germany, the United States boasted 1,273 breweries, and of them 1,250 were microbrewers—up from 8 in 1980.

Why did microbreweries start proliferating in the 1980s? An important piece of the puzzle was the legalization by the US Congress of home brewing, on February 1, 1979. This legislation legitimated a movement that had been gaining steam for several years. By 1984, the American Homebrewers Association had 3,000 members and its goal was to democratize the production of beer. It assailed the stranglehold of the leading US beer producers. Their "industrial beer"—disparaged as thin and overcarbonated—was the hot cause of the microbrew movement.

In addition to exacerbating discontent among beer aficionados about the lack of choice and the dearth of fresh, tasteful beer sold at bars, restaurants, and other gathering places, the home-brewing movement educated consumers about traditional beers and artisanal techniques. Brewing, frequenting brew-pubs, and attending beer festivals became forms of cool mobilization. In 1982, Bert Grant opened the first brew-pub in Yakima, Washington. That same year, the Great American Beer Festival drew about 40 brewers and 700 beer enthusiasts.

The passion to make tasteful beer with traditional artisanal techniques induced more microbrewers and brew-pub owners to enter the industry. Their spirit was exemplified by Bob Connor of the Independence Brewing Company, whose billboard read: "Independence—enjoy it while it lasts." As Anchor Brewing owner Fritz Maytag put it in an interview, "The more breweries there are, the more it will help all of us. Alone we mean nothing, but if there are a lot of us, we can make a difference." The number of new microbreweries and brewpubs increased in tandem: microbrews and brew-pubs legitimized each other and enhanced each other's cultural acceptance.

By 1994, close to 500 establishments were part of the $400 million craft beer movement in the United States. Although microbrewers crafted more than two million barrels of beer, their revenues were much lower than those generated by Michelob Light. Microbreweries and brewpubs weren't about volume: they were an expression of a new identity, one premised on small-scale, authentic, and traditional

methods of production, and fresh beer with myriad tastes.

Rebels in opposition: Biotechnology commercialization

In 1972, Germany's Federal Research Ministry established a national biotech-nology laboratory to promote research. By the early 1980s, Germans were apply-ing for more biotechnology patents than Americans were. However, by 1990 German pharmaceutical companies either had plants sitting idle (like Hoechst AG's $37 million facility in Frankfurt) or had delayed construction of new ones. Meanwhile, 75 percent of German biotechnology investments flowed past German borders, especially to the United States. BASF established a lab in Massachusetts; Bayer and Henkel targeted California. What happened?

For starters, German antibiotech activists made their cause a hot one by depicting biotechnology as a Faustian bargain that risked resurrecting Nazi eugenics and genetic discrimination. This emotional appeal enabled a small group of core activists to recruit a wide range of allies and sympathizers such as workers within pharmaceu-tical companies, schoolteachers, neighbors of scientists, church groups and leaders, politicians across the political spectrum, and part of the scientific community.

By reducing biotechnology to genetic engineering and connecting it to Nazi eugenics, the antibiotech activists made biotechnology a matter of basic principles and a technology imbued with "incalculable risk," a term borrowed from the parallel debate about nuclear energy. As early as 1984–85, a parlia-mentary commission entrusted with writing a report on biotechnology titled it, "Opportunities and Risks of Genetic Technology." By contrast, the Office of Technology Assessment in the United States released a report titled *Commercial Biotechnology*, which reviewed the economic prospects of the technology and how the federal government could support the industry.

At the same time, activists in Germany fostered cool mobilization. To arouse public concern, they held protests at large physical structures, such as corporate fermentation plants, rather than small university laboratories. Protests and marches often were local exercises, and activists staged dramatic spectacles to garner TV coverage and make the dangers of biotechnology more vivid: headless chickens strutting before demonstrations, disabled protestors holding signs against reproductive genetic screening, and deformed mutant mice in animal-testing cages. Emotion-laden tactics left the pharmaceutical companies reeling because they relied on a strategy of presenting "facts." As one public relations veteran confessed:

> I went to a panel at the nearest high school with a Green member of the state parliament. There were 500 people in attendance and it was packed. I was winning the argument, and suddenly [my opponent] started to scream and cry. So I said to her, "Don't you think we should stop being so emotional and be more objective about this?" At that point a 50-year-old lady in the audience stood up and said, "Are you only a brain or do you actually have a heart in this issue too?"

The challenges and delaying tactics of activists created uncertainty regard-ing both the future of regulation and the speed with which companies could bring products to market, effects that had serious implications for likely returns on investment. As one executive noted, "The question often was, 'Why spend money on this biotech thing, where we may make some money in ten years or not, when we could spend it on a chemical product or a product line extension, where we can make money within two or three years?'" By shaping the terms of this debate, market rebels inhibited biotech commercialization efforts in Germany.

Thinking like an insurgent

Social movements represent a double-edged sword for companies. Capitalizing on preexisting movements can create enormous opportunities. Nike, for example, owes its early success—indeed, its existence—to the running movement powered by Oregon track coach Bill Bowerman and doctor Kenneth Cooper (who pioneered aerobics) to athletes like Frank Shorter and to a network of running clubs that dotted the country.

But social movements also pose threats. The antitobacco movement drew on a coalition of health researchers and attorneys who played a central role in placing restrictions on the market for cigarettes. Similarly, the organic-food movement, which emphasizes an alliance between environmentalists and proponents of locally available foods, has created a formidable challenge for food companies purveying standardized products.

The challenge for managers is to start thinking like insurgents, which for many will require effecting a serious mindset shift. As the examples below emphasize, executives who are able to do so boost their odds not only of shaping market acceptance of innovative products but also of stimulating radical change, when it is needed, inside their own organizations.

From deliberate cognition to automatic cognition

Many managers rely on deliberate cognition—that is, the ability of the human mind to process and analyze information—and an appeal to reason. By contrast, insurgents realize that audiences rely on automatic cognition, or shortcuts, to make sense of the world. Hence, they use symbols to communicate their point of view. Nissan's Carlos Ghosn employed this approach when he took over the dispirited company.[1] Ghosn initially spent two months walking the halls. He found that while line workers knew how *long* it took to build a car, they did not know how much it *cost* to build a car. And when he asked Nissan dealers, "Who's your biggest competitor?" he was shocked to hear their answer: "The Nissan dealer down the street."

Such findings convinced Ghosn that far-reaching social and emotional mobilization was necessary to turn Nissan around. The first change he made, therefore, was symbolic: English would be the company's language. It was a shock to the whole organization, and Ghosn's way of seizing neutral ground. He wanted to signal that Nissan was a global company—not a French or Japanese one—and to highlight transparency: no interpreters, no translation. Soon all employees received a small dictionary that defined key terms like "target" and "performance." The point was to make being a global company more than just rhetoric. The introduction of English was the first step in a social movement to restore pride and innovation at Nissan.

From information to emotions

Managers believe in disseminating information. Insurgents realize that emotions of pride and anger are essential to "unfreeze" and move inert organizations forward. One organization that has used emotion to effect change is Gujarat Gas (an affiliate of British Gas), which supplies gas services to a small city in India. The managing director wanted to make the organization into a customer-focused enterprise, but it was a group of activists—young, mid-level managers with a fierce commitment to change—who led the charge. They believed that being responsive to the customer didn't mean doing something *to* a customer, it meant doing something *with* customers.

To persuade others, they made employees go through the experience of being a customer. The employees were sent outside the company office and learned when they sought to visit the office that they had to run a series of gauntlets: first, the sentry at the gate who interrogated them and made them wait; then several clerks delayed things. Who played the role of the sentry and clerks? Customers! Following the role play, employees and customers came together in a large room, and all 400 narrated their experiences. Articulating these experiences amplified the moral shock felt by employees—the shock of self-recognition.

From one-way to two-way communication

Many managers prefer one-way communication; thus, they organize road

[1] See Kathryn Hughes, Jean-Louis Barsoux, and Jean-François Manzoni, "Redesigning Nissan: Carlos Ghosn takes charge," case study, INSEAD, 2003.

shows and town hall meetings in which they unveil PowerPoint presentations. Insurgents rely on two-way communication. They reverse the structure of the town hall; the audience asks questions and becomes engaged. Managers can try this online through "jams," or giant conversations. IBM has had several online jams featuring thousands of employees. In the Values Jam, 320,000 employees weighed in over a 72-hour period. The values that emerged—dedication to clients, innovation that matters, and trust—gained currency because they were crafted through mass mobilization, rather than being chosen and transmitted by executives.

From roll-out to WUNC

Most managers are concerned with rolling out a change and preoccupied with overcoming resistance to it. Insurgents go where there is energy and are concerned with drawing in people. By getting their audiences to do things collectively, insurgents sustain emotion and foster worthiness, unity, numbers, and commitment (WUNC—a term coined by Charles Tilly to describe the source of strength for social movements). Feelings of worthiness and unity, along with large numbers of committed members willing to take collective risks, are essential if a movement is to have impact.

Consider PSS World Medical, a company that provides medical supplies to physician practices through its network of drivers and warehouses.[2] It believes in open-book management and recognizes that employees "fire" bosses by disengaging emotionally from the business. When it acquired a company called Taylor Medical in Dallas, Texas, the PSS World Medical manager in charge of integration, Gary Corliss, asked Taylor employees to join him for an all-hands meeting to discuss PSS values. The first question he asked employees was, "Tell me everything you hate here." As he suspected, they pointed to cameras that the Taylor warehouse manager had installed to monitor employees and deter theft. Corliss, who had walked into the meeting with a baseball bat, smashed the camera, and invited others to do the same (with a blanket to protect them from shards of glass). Employees then destroyed the cameras. This cathartic act enabled them to express pent-up emotions and have a conversation about cultural change. Within six months, turnover—which had been a problem— fell to zero.

Market rebels aren't Molotov cocktail–throwing World Trade Organization opponents. They are groups of individuals who together shape markets through hot causes, which arouse emotions, and through cool mobilization, which allows participants to realize collective identities. Executives that understand the roles and practices of market rebels are more likely to be successful innovation leaders. Q

This article is adapted from Hayagreeva Rao's book *Market Rebels: How Activists Make or Break Radical Innovations* (New Jersey: Princeton University Press, 2009). Copyright © 2009 McKinsey & Company. All rights reserved.

We welcome your comments on this article. Please send them to quarterly_comments@ mckinsey.com.

[2] See Charles O'Reilly and Jeffrey Pfeffer, "PSS World Medical: The challenges of growth and the financial markets," case study, Stanford University Graduate School of Business, 1999.

In Response

Comments from invited experts

The McKinsey Quarterly, 2008 Number 4, and mckinseyquarterly.com featured the essay "What China can learn from Japan on cleaning up the environment," by Bill Emmott, former editor of the *Economist*. Three experts on Asia were invited to comment on the article; we present their observations below, followed by Emmott's response.

Richard Katz:

Bill Emmott rightly suggests, in "What China can learn from Japan on cleaning up the environment," that China can learn from Japan's experience in combining high growth and environmental protection. During the boom years of the 1960s, Japan's emissions of pollutants (such as nitrogen dioxide, carbon monoxide, and sulfur dioxide) tripled, primarily because the country began to consume more oil. In those years, Japanese cities were the most polluted in the world. For years, the ruling Liberal Democratic Party (LDP), on behalf of its business allies, quashed efforts to improve air quality.

Two factors forced change: a political backlash and a global oil shock. The LDP increasingly lost its popularity in the cities, where more and more people lived. By the end of the 1960s, support for the LDP was at a low; many analysts warned that it was on the verge of losing control of the legislature. In 1970, party leaders in the so-called Pollution Diet pushed through stringent pollution controls in a bid to regain popularity. The 1973 oil embargo provoked an immediate sense of crisis in Japan, which depended on imports for virtually all the petroleum it consumed. Almost overnight, high oil prices triggered an enormous balance of payments problem and wreaked havoc in the domestic economy. Japan responded with sweeping conservation measures and a nationwide push to switch from oil to other sources of energy. Together, these two developments reduced Japanese air pollution levels at a rate unprecedented in any other industrialized society. Japanese sulfur emissions, for example, declined by almost 90 percent.

Richard Katz is an economist and editor of the Oriental Economist's *semiweekly TOE Alert, as well as the author of* Japan, the System That Soured: The Rise and Fall of the Japanese Economic Miracle.

The Japanese experience suggests that democracy is a positive, not a negative, factor in forcing political leaders to come to grips with environmental problems. On a visit to China this past May, I met with some residents in the southwestern city of Chengdu. They told me of their plans to participate in a "stroll" to protest the construction of a petrochemical plant that was closer to the city than permitted under national environmental regulations. As with the LDP in the 1960s, local leaders were more concerned with immediate GDP growth and tax revenue than with public health and sustainable growth. Three days before the stroll, leaders of the event were arrested. Central-government officials who profess genuine concern about the degradation of China's environment say that their efforts to combat pollution are often thwarted by resistance from local potentates.

Nonetheless, we shouldn't lose sight of the fact that China has made real progress in improving its environmental record. Over the past quarter century, the country's carbon dioxide emissions per dollar of real GDP have plunged by a stunning two-thirds. Industry-caused water pollution per worker peaked in 1989 and has come down 8 percent since. The Chinese government reports that in 2005, forests covered 18 percent of the Chinese landmass, up from 14 percent in 1993. The construction of treatment plants and the more rigorous enforcement of penalties on discharges have steadily improved water quality. Today, according to the World Bank, about 60 percent of the rivers in China's south have Class I–II water quality (suitable for drinking), compared with none in 1990.

The problem is that China is so big and growing so fast that these efforts aren't enough. Even if pollution per dollar of GDP goes down, the absolute level of pollution is still rising rapidly. Today, China's emissions of greenhouse gases per dollar of GDP are 68 percent lower than they were in 1980. But because GDP is so much larger, total emissions have surged 240 percent. And progress varies widely by region. In the water-scarce north—home to 42 percent of China's people—half of the rivers no longer sustain fish or plant life.

No environmental solution will work if it means telling the Chinese people that they must stay poor. On a recent visit to Yunnan province, representatives from the Nature Conservancy showed us how families in the Himalayan village of Meiquan had used support from that US-based environmental group and the Chinese government to install indoor plumbing, solar-powered water heaters, and methane gas cookers fueled by animal waste. The result: families no longer have to spend a third of their work year cutting down trees and hauling water, so they have more time for raising cash crops, get fewer diseases from inhaling the smoke produced by wood-burning stoves, and suffer less soil erosion. The challenge for China will be to replicate this combination—an increase in both living standards and environmental protection—on a nationwide scale. •

Minxin Pei:

Environmental degradation leads the list of potential threats to the sustainability of China's rapid growth. Can the country manage this threat? Optimists such as former *Economist* editor Bill Emmott contend that it is up to the challenge. To hear him tell the story, a wise and powerful bureaucracy, reinforced by security forces, will give China inherent advantages in grappling with these problems. High growth, he suggests, has filled the government's coffers, leaving it with ample revenue to finance sweeping new environmental-protection measures.

Minxin Pei is a senior associate at the Carnegie Endowment for International Peace, in Washington, DC, and the author of *China's Trapped Transition: The Limits of Developmental Autocracy* (2006).

There's no denying the strength of the Chinese state. When its leaders resolve to fix a problem, they can mobilize extraordinary administrative and financial resources to accomplish feats that inspire awe around the world. The success of the Beijing Olympic Games and China's recent manned space flight are only the latest examples of this ability to achieve big things in little time. But cleaning up the environment is a different kind of challenge, with costs vastly higher than those of hosting a sports extravaganza or launching an astronaut. China's leaders are unlikely to elevate environmental degradation to top-priority status unless they see it as a matter of national security or, more to the point, as an issue that threatens the Communist Party's rule.

These leaders clearly recognize the danger of continued environmental destruction and wish to do something about it. What's not clear is whether they see it as so significant that it warrants accepting slower rates of economic growth. While there is relatively little consensus among them about how much of a threat continued environmental damage poses to the government, they do agree that slower growth poses a clear and present danger to it.

Economic growth, rather than environmental stewardship, therefore remains the most important criterion in evaluating the performance of local officials. However powerful the Chinese bureaucracy, its officials probably won't implement environmentally friendly edicts from on high. In any case, Beijing has shown itself to be of two minds about the trade-off between growth and the environment. Four years ago, the government sanctioned a study[1] to estimate the cost of environmental damage. The report showed that pollution generated health costs and physical damage equal to 5.8 percent of GDP and that about 750,000 people a year die prematurely because of air and water pollution. The government received the news so badly that the study was quickly called off.

Beijing demonstrated its environmental ambivalence again in an administrative-restructuring effort announced in March 2008. The environmental-protection agency did become a ministry. Yet its elevation was mostly cosmetic because local environmental bureaucracies, the greater part of the whole, remained outside its control and answerable to local governments—the principal culprits in the crisis.

As to financial resources, the amount of new investment required merely to make up for the accumulated underinvestment would be substantial. A study conducted in 2004 by the then State Environmental Protection Administration (now the Ministry of Environmental Protection) suggests that China ought to spend 2.4 percent of its GDP a year on treating air, water, and solid-waste pollution. Actual government spending for these purposes comes to only 0.6 percent of GDP, implying underinvestment of 1.8 percent of GDP a year. The same study concludes that "if all the pollutants discharged in 2004 are treated using existing technologies, the one-time investment required is 1,080 billion yuan [about $150 billion], or 6.8 percent of GDP."[2]

The most difficult hurdles, however, are political, not economic. Japan tackled these problems successfully because it has a free press and, compared with China, a competitive political system. The enforcement of environmental rules requires not only powerful bureaucracies but also, and perhaps more important, a vigilant media and aggressive civic groups. Tight restrictions on these forces hobble China's effort to enforce stricter rules. To be sure, the country is much freer today than it was 30 years ago. Nongovernmental organizations have begun to play a more visible role in fighting environmental degradation. Even the press has grown bolder in reporting on it. These are encouraging developments, but so far they have had only a modest impact on the Chinese state's environmental performance.

---

[1] See "Cost of pollution in China: Economic estimates of physical damages," *The World Bank*, February 2007.
[2] See *China Green National Accounting Study Report 2004*, State Environmental Protection Administration of China and National Bureau of Statistics of China, 2006.

Until the government changes its priorities and loosens its grip on the media and civil society, China will have a hard time reversing or even halting the wholesale destruction of the environment. There will be occasional victories, bursts of progress here and there, but the overall picture will look nothing like the bold gains imagined in China's official rhetoric—or in Bill Emmott's optimistic predictions. •

Andrew Grant:

Bill Emmott is right to observe that as China wrestles with the environmental consequences of economic development, the country can profit from studying the successes of its Asian neighbors. But in many ways, the nation whose environmental challenges have the greatest relevance for China is the United States, not Japan.

Like the United States, China is a big country whose population centers and resources are widely dispersed. Japan, by contrast, is a mountainous island nation smaller than the state of California. China's population is ten times larger than Japan's, and its people occupy a space 30 times larger. China's population density, 138 people per square kilometer (0.39 square miles), is only a third of Japan's, at 339 people per square kilometer, and the averages understate the difference, because about half of Japan's 127 million people are crowded into just two cities, Tokyo and Osaka. The leading cities of China, Beijing and Shanghai, account for less than 3 percent of its population.

Given China's large size and moderate population density, it's not hard to understand why the country's leaders would share America's passion for cars and highways rather than Japan's affinity for subways and bullet trains. As you'd expect, China is barreling ahead with the development of its auto industry. Already, it has eclipsed Japan as the world's second-largest auto market and, at current growth rates, will overtake the United States as the largest one by 2030. It's sobering to contemplate the environmental implications should China, which now has about 30 cars for every 1,000 people of driving age, seek to emulate the United States, with its 900 cars per thousand people of driving age.

Another crucial similarity between the United States and China: both have abundant reserves of coal. Indeed, China is the world's largest producer, with 2007 output topping 2.5 billion metric tons, or about 40 percent of the global total. (The United States, which produced 17 percent of the world's coal, was a distant second; Japan has no significant coal deposits.) For China's economy, coal is a blessing because it's so much less expensive than petroleum, nuclear power, or alternative energy sources, such as wind and solar. But from an environmental perspective, a ready supply of coal can be a curse: even the relatively clean varieties generate about 25 and 80 percent more carbon than gasoline and natural gas, respectively. Coal-rich and coal-poor economies face starkly different development trade-offs. Little wonder that coal accounts for 70 percent of China's total energy consumption and nuclear power for less than 3 percent (in Japan, coal's share of total energy consumed is only 20 percent, and nuclear power, at 13 percent, is economically competitive). Beijing has pledged to reduce China's reliance on coal to 60 percent of energy consumption within ten years. But coal is sure to remain a powerful temptation, especially in periods of below-trend growth.

Andrew Grant is a director in McKinsey's Shanghai office.

A third way China resembles the United States more than Japan is the decentralized nature of China's environmental regulatory system. During Japan's high-growth years, powerful bureaucrats in the Ministry of International Trade and Industry or other organs of the central government wrote and enforced energy and environmental policies. In China, policy goals are set in Beijing, but enforcement falls largely to local officials, many of whom regard growth as a more urgent priority than green. The virtue of China's decentralized system is that it allows for local innovation. Officials in Dalian, on China's northeastern coast, have shown that concern for the environment doesn't have to come at the expense of jobs and higher living standards. But Beijing must do more to showcase such successes and encourage leaders in other areas to emulate them.

The good news is that while many of China's environmental challenges resemble those facing the United States, China's leaders have shown a greater willingness than their US counterparts to explore creative solutions. China has embraced many successful strategies of its Asian neighbors and devised innovative environmental responses of its own. Consider transportation policy, where China is combining its effort to develop a domestic auto industry with an ambitious mass-transit agenda. Currently, the country is building large mass-transit systems in ten major cities. More will be needed. We estimate that China will have to construct 100 to 170 mass-transit systems within the next 15 years to have one in all cities large enough to benefit. Still, the country is off to an impressive start.

Beijing also is channeling resources to environmentally friendly technologies, such as wind and solar power (under the government's current targets, renewable energy will account for 15 percent of total energy consumption by 2015). We believe China has a unique opportunity to establish global leadership in the development of several alternative-energy technologies, including electric vehicles. (Warren Buffet appears to share our optimism: Berkshire Hathaway recently invested $350 million in BYD, a leading Chinese battery maker set to begin mass production of electric cars next year.) In nuclear energy, too, China aims to develop its own technology to meet domestic market requirements: Beijing has announced plans to build 32 new reactors by 2020, quadrupling the current number. We also expect ample funding for green technologies in the government's recently announced economic-stimulus package.

Urban planning will play a crucial role in determining the magnitude of China's energy and environmental challenge. The country's urban population, we estimate, will swell to 925 million people by 2025, up from 600 million today. This is a demographic shift without precedent in human civilization. The McKinsey Global Institute has modeled a variety of scenarios for such a huge urban influx. It found that if the government encouraged the development of a handful of megacities complementing scattered, less densely populated urban centers—a strategy we call "concentrated growth"—annual energy consumption and carbon emissions could be as much as 20 percent lower than they will be if the country continues on its current course. By our estimates, a concentrated-growth strategy could mean that China's energy requirements will be the equivalent of 1.5 million barrels of oil a day lower than they would be if the country opts instead for dispersed urbanization.

China's leaders recognize these opportunities—and the costs of failing to seize them. They deserve credit for their determination to embrace the best practices of other nations and to formulate unique Chinese solutions for sustainable growth. That blend of inventiveness and pragmatism bodes well for China's ability to rise to the magnitude of the task at hand. •

Bill Emmott responds:

All countries are different: that is what makes studying them and working in them interesting. So are historical periods: we do move on and things do change, whatever George Santayana might have said about knowing history to avoid repeating mistakes. Nevertheless, if we are careful, acknowledging all the genuine differences, comparisons between countries and historical experience can provide some enlightenment.

So it is, I would argue, with China and Japan in the matter of the environment. They are of different sizes, with different political systems, and the energy business of the 1960s and 1970s was different from today's. The essential point, though, is that Japan then, like China now, faced the need to reconcile its fast industrial growth with the social and political effects of environmental degradation. Many who look at China now, breathing its air and smelling its water, throw up their hands in despair and then extend that despair to the global issue of climate change. The way Japan transformed itself from champion dirt producer to one of the industrial world's cleanest countries should at least temper that despair. Solutions can be found and trade-offs changed.

Bill Emmott is the former editor of the *Economist* and author of *Rivals: How the Power Struggle Between China, India and Japan Will Shape Our Next Decade.*

But will they and, if so, how? Minxin Pei misinterprets me if he thinks I am a starry-eyed optimist about the magical powers of the Chinese autocracy. But he also misinterprets Japan if he thinks a free press and an active civil society really wrought the miracle there. They played their part, as Richard Katz eloquently describes, but they took an enormously long time to do so. Minamata disease, for example, was first clearly ascribed to the Chisso Corporation's mercury discharges in 1959. Yet discharges continued for a further nine years, and legal battles over compensation for those killed and maimed went on until 1995.

The question, really, is whether public pressure in China for stricter environmental controls can find an identity of interest with a desire in the central government to clean things up. Public opinion does matter in China and does find ways to express itself, despite the lack of a free media. Still, it seems to make a difference principally when the central government chooses to enter into a sort of alliance with public pressure against local officials. China, as Andrew Grant says, is decentralized in a way that Japan is not. This does not, however, mean that the central government never gets its way.

What we have to look for are indicators that the central government feels a need to get serious about an environmental cleanup. Some of these indicators may well actually be signs that, like the Liberal Democratic Party in Japan after 1970, it feels obliged to get serious for fear of its own survival. Right now, that fear is likelier to emanate from unemployment and the economic downturn than from pollution. But that will not always be true. *Q*

Enduring Ideas

Classic McKinsey frameworks that continue to inform management thinking

The business system

Technology-based manufacturing example

Technology	Product design	Manufacturing	Marketing	Distribution	Service
• Patents • Product, process choices • Sophistication • Source	• Aesthetics • Function • Physical characteristics • Quality	• Capacity • Integration • Location • Raw materials	• Advertising, promotion • Brand • Packaging • Prices • Sales force	• Channels • Integration • Inventory • Transport • Warehousing	• Captive vs independent providers • Pricing • Speed • Warranty

Business strategy involves an integrated set of actions designed to help companies gain sustainable advantage over competitors. The business system is a framework that allows a company to formulate the set of actions most likely to achieve this advantage. First introduced in a McKinsey staff paper in 1980,[1] the business system was later presented to the public by McKinsey's Fred Gluck,[2] who stressed its usefulness in forming strategy. In 1985, Harvard's Michael Porter introduced a similar framework—the value chain—and cited the business system concept in the book *Competitive Advantage*.[3]

The business system charts all the steps involved in creating and delivering a company's product. At each link in the chain, managers have a choice of how to conduct business. From a strategic point of view, the most important assessment is how the choices made at each step reinforce the company's overall value proposition, and hence, its competitive advantage.

To develop improvements to any one link, managers can ask a series of open-ended questions about current practices and alternate possibilities: How does the company perform at this stage? Is there a better way? How do competitors behave? Who achieves lower costs? By varying the questions, examining scenarios, and evaluating all in light of the company's total strategy, a company can discover new strategic moves to make within an existing business—for example, whether to expand or diversify. When used to evaluate acquisitions, the framework forces managers to look for synergies between the target's own activities and the company's current business system.

A surprisingly simple concept, the business system continues to be a serviceable tool. Deeper examination of current conditions and potential changes at each stage can reveal the forces likely to shape a business over time—and the competitive capabilities required to meet them.

[1] Carter F. Bales, P. C. Chatterjee, Donald Gogel, and Anupam Puri, "Competitive cost analysis," McKinsey & Company, March 1980.

[2] Frederick W. Gluck, "Strategic choices and research allocation," *The McKinsey Quarterly*, 1980 Number 1, pp. 22–33.

[3] Michael Porter, *Competitive Advantage: Creating and Sustaining Superior Performance*, New York: Free Press, 1985.